PREACHING
MARK

Talk outlines for Mark's Gospel

Preaching Mark

This book combines volumes 1 and 2, previously published in 2006 and 2007
© Phil Crowter/The Good Book Company 2009

Published by
The Good Book Company Ltd
Elm House, 37 Elm Road
New Malden, Surrey KT3 3HB, UK
email: ppp@thegoodbook.co.uk
UK: www.thegoodbook.co.uk
USA & Canada: www.thegoodbook.com
Australia: www.thegoodbook.com.au

ISBN: 9781905564514

Printed in India

The *Pray Prepare Preach* project is working in partnership with a growing number of organisations worldwide, including:
Langham Partnership
Grace Baptist Mission
Pastor Training International (PTI)
Sovereign World Trust
Africa Inland Mission (AIM)
Worldshare
Entrust Foundation
India Bible Literature

African Pastors' Book Fund
Preacher's Help
African Christian Textbooks (ACTS) Nigeria
Orphans for Christ, Uganda
Project Timothy

Also in this series:
Preaching God's Big Picture

Coming soon:
Preaching Philippians
Preaching Job

Please read this first!

We preachers have the best job in the world!

The word of God gives life to dead people. The word of God feeds hungry people. The word of God brings Jesus to us.

And we teach this word of God!

2 Timothy 2:15 says: *'Be a good worker, one who does not need to be ashamed, one who correctly (rightly) explains the word of truth.'* (NLT)

Preaching Mark will help you to do this. It will help you to:

- **Understand** what Mark tells us about Jesus Christ.
- **Think** how each section is important for your people.
- **Teach** the main point clearly.

Each section of *Preaching Mark* helps you to **study** and **preach** part of Mark's Gospel. You still have to work hard! We have given you some help, some ideas. You need to ask God to help you to explain those truths to your people.

Here is the best way to use this book. **Start at the beginning of Mark and teach each section in turn**. Then your people will understand how Mark tells his Jesus story.

We have the best job in the world. Do it well – with God's help!

Before you start, take time to read:
A. **Quick Help:** How to prepare a talk on Mark
B. How to use *Preaching Mark*.
C. About the Gospel of Mark

You can see an example of how to use *Preaching Mark* in Section E at the end of the book.

Phil Crowter

CONTENTS

A. QUICK HELP:
How to prepare a talk on Mark

1. Pray for God's help

2. 📖 Read the Bible section several times.
Use ⊙ **Background** to help you to understand the section.
Use ⊙ **Notes** to help you to understand difficult Bible verses.

3. Try to find the main point that God is teaching us in the Bible section.
Use ⊙ **Main point** to help you.

4. Pray for your people. Think how this Bible section will help them.
Use ⊠ **Something to work on** to help you

5. Write your talk in your own language. Start with the main points which the Bible teaches.
Use our notes in the **PREACH** section to help you.

6. Now write a beginning and an end for your talk.

7. Check what you have done.
- Is the **main point** clear?
- Do you show them what the **Bible** teaches?
- Do you use **word pictures** to help your people understand and remember?
- Do you **connect** with the people?
- What do you hope will **change**?

8. Pray that God will speak through your words. Pray that his truth will change people.

For more help read the next section.

B. How to use Preaching Mark

Every time you prepare a talk, begin with these things:

- Pray for God's help.

- Read the Bible section.

- Try to find the main point that God is teaching us in the Bible section.

Then you can use these notes to help you. There are two pages for each talk. The first page helps you to think about the Bible section. The second page gives you headings and ideas for a talk.

When you see this symbol  , you need to read what the Bible says.

STUDY PAGE:
Understand the Bible

The first page helps you to understand the Bible section.

⊙ **BACKGROUND**: It is very important to think about what comes before and after the section. We will look at a few verses each time. However, those verses fit into Mark's big story about Jesus. Always ask how a section is like other things in Mark. Ask how it helps us to understand who Jesus is and why Jesus came.

The **Background** section will help you to do this.

⊙ **MAIN POINT**: We have put the most important point in a few words. Think about this point. Can you see this is what the Bible section is teaching? Try to make sure that this point is very clear in your talk.

⊡ **SOMETHING TO WORK ON**: This part chooses something from the Bible section which you need to think about. It is important to work hard to understand the Bible. Think carefully about how to teach the point in this section. We may use a word picture to help you.

⊙ **NOTES**: This section tells you about difficult Bible verses. It will help you not to make mistakes when you are teaching.

9

PREACH PAGE:
Teach the Bible

The second page helps you to teach the Bible section. You must also do your own work. This page gives you ideas. You must take the ideas and use them in the best way. We give you the bones, but you must put the meat on the bones!

1. THINGS WE HAVE WRITTEN TO HELP YOU

• Two or three headings. **THESE ARE WRITTEN LIKE THIS.** These headings will help you to teach the Bible clearly. You can change the headings to make them better for your people.

• **We show you what the Bible says.** We want people to listen to the Bible. Keep reminding them of what the Bible says. If they have a Bible, ask them to find the verse you are talking about. This symbol 📖 will help you know when to do this.

• **We explain what the Bible is teaching.** You need to think how to explain the Bible so that your people understand. You know your people. We do not know your people. Your words are better than our words.

• **We sometimes use a word picture.** Here is an example from the notes on Mark 1:16-20.

⊕ **Imagine this.** *You see someone who is busy at work. He has a good job. He has a house and a family to look after. You tell him to leave his work and follow you. You will not pay him money. What will he tell you to do? He will tell you to go away! But when Jesus says 'Follow me', what happens?*

The word picture may not be good for your people. In your village, people may not have jobs which bring money. A Bible teacher must find a better word picture to help the people understand. You will need to find many more word pictures to help teach the Bible truth. Be very careful that the word picture teaches what the Bible is saying.

• **We show you how to connect the Bible teaching to your people.** It is important to hear God's word speaking **to us.** We need to know how the Bible teaching changes us. Here is an example:

> ⊗ *We have the best news to tell! Think of people who have not heard the good news about Jesus. How will you tell them?*

- **We give you one or two ideas.** You need to think of more ways to connect the Bible to your people. You know the people. You know how the Bible needs to change their lives.

2. OTHER THINGS YOU WILL NEED TO DO

- **Think how to start your talk.** Your people need to see why it is important to listen today. Tell them what you will teach them from the Bible. Tell them why it is important for them.

- **Think how to end your talk.** Remind them of the main points. Give them something to think about, or something to do.

- **Pray!** You are telling the people God's truth from God's word. Pray that God will use your words to speak to the people. Pray that God's truth will change people.

- **Always use your own language. Never** say things in English, if the people do not speak English well.

If you need further help, we have shown how to prepare a talk from this book. Turn to the end, and you will see an example of how to use this book to Preach Mark!

C. About the Gospel of Mark

1. WHO WROTE IT?

Mark wrote it. Mark was not one of the 12 disciples. He is probably 'John Mark', who we read about in **Acts 12:12, 25** and other places. Probably, **Peter** told Mark all the things that happened. Then Mark wrote them down in his Gospel.

2. WHEN DID MARK WRITE IT?

Most likely between A.D. 40 and A.D. 65. So, Mark is the **earliest** Gospel. Matthew and Luke use parts of Mark's Gospel. This is why some sections in Matthew and Luke are the same as Mark.

3. WHY DID MARK WRITE IT?

Mark tells us why he wrote it, in **Mark 1:1**. *'The beginning of the gospel about Jesus Christ, the Son of God.'*

He tells us the **good news** ('gospel') of Jesus Christ. Mark's Gospel is not just the life story of Jesus. It is about the good news of:

• who Jesus is
• why Jesus came
• why Jesus died.

This is Mark's big message.

Remembering this will help us to understand the stories about Jesus. Mark does not tell these stories just so that we know what happened. Mark has a better reason. He tells us the stories about Jesus to **help us understand** who Jesus is and why he came. He wants us to repent and believe (Mark 1:15).

Remember this big message when you preach Mark's Gospel. The stories all fit together. They have a message. Mark's Gospel is the big message about Jesus, not lots of different stories.

So, when we preach on one story, we ask ourselves questions like this –

• *Why does Mark put this story in? How does it fit?*

• *What does it tell us about who Jesus is, or why Jesus came?*

• *How does it help us to trust in Jesus?*

4. WHAT IS MARK'S PLAN?

Mark divides his Gospel into two halves.

• WHO JESUS IS; Mark 1-8

• WHY JESUS CAME; Mark 9-16

WHO JESUS IS	WHY JESUS CAME
Mark chapters 1-8	Mark chapters 9-16

Mark 1-8 is about who Jesus is. Jesus is the Christ, the Son of God, Mark 1:1; 2:7; 4:41; 8:29.

Mark 9-16 is about why Jesus came. Jesus came to suffer and die for sins, Mark 10:45.

Try to remember this plan. It will help you to understand Mark.

You can see the two halves in
📖 **Mark 8:29, 31.**

In Mark 1-8, Jesus has shown the disciples many times who he is. But they have not understood. At last, in Mark 8:29 Peter sees who Jesus is! Jesus immediately starts to teach his disciples why he came (Mark 8:31). But the disciples do not understand that Jesus must die. So, as Jesus goes towards Jerusalem and the cross, he teaches the disciples that he came to die (Mark 9-16).

PREACHING
MARK

D. Study and Preach Mark's Gospel

1 THE GOOD NEWS ABOUT JESUS CHRIST

▣ Background

📖 *Mark 1:1-15.* This section is Mark's **start** or **introduction** to his book. It tells us the main point of his book. Notice that John and Jesus preach the same message. When we have read about Jesus Christ, we too should 'repent and believe the good news'.

▣ Main point

Jesus Christ has come as God promised. This is good news. We should come to Jesus and repent.

▣ Something to work on

1. **Pray that God will help you show people how important and wonderful Jesus is.** Mark's good news is Jesus, so we must preach Jesus!

2. **Make sure that they understand 'repent' ('turn away from your sins').** Mark 1:4, 15. 'Repent' means more than 'say sorry'.

When we repent we turn round. We change our mind. We do not go sin's way any longer. We go God's way. Use a word picture to help.

▣ Notes

• **Mark 1:2, 3.** Mark uses the words of Isaiah 40:3. He shows that John is the 'messenger' (prophet) that Isaiah told people about. Isaiah uses a picture. A person is making a good road, ready for the King to ride on. John is like this person.

• **Mark 1:6.** John is dressed like the prophet Elijah (2 Kings 1:8).

• **Mark 1:7.** John is talking about Jesus. Crowds of people listen to John, but he does not feel important. Jesus is much more important than he is.

• **Mark 1:8.** John can only make people wet. Jesus will wash people from their sin. Jesus will change people by his Holy Spirit. This verse talks about what happens when Jesus makes us a Christian. 📖 *Read 1 Corinthians 12:13.*

THE GOOD NEWS

📖 *Mark 1:1-3*

1. JESUS CHRIST IS THE GOOD NEWS

In Mark 1:1 'gospel' means 'good news'. The good news is a **person**! Usually good news is when some**thing** happens. But the best news is when this **person** comes. God had promised this person for hundreds of years. Isaiah the prophet spoke about him (Mark 2:2, 3).

• **Jesus is the Christ (Mark 1:1).** 'Christ' is not just another name that Jesus has. It is his **job**. Jesus' job is to be the 'Christ' or **king** that God sent. Think how excited you would be if the most powerful ruler in the world came to see you! Jesus is far more important, because he is the king of **heaven**.

• **Jesus is God's Son (Mark 1:1).** When we truly believe that Jesus is God's Son, we will bow and worship him. We will believe everything he says. We will give our lives to him.

• **Jesus came to wash us clean inside. (Mark 1:8).** Jesus did not come to punish us for our sin! Jesus came to forgive us! This is why John 'baptised' people (dipped people in water). He baptised people to show that Jesus was coming to wash them from their sin.

2. TELL THE GOOD NEWS!

When you have good news, you do not keep quiet. You tell people about it! *[Think of an example.]* God gave John a job to do. He must tell people the good news about Jesus.

📖 *Mark 1:2-4, 7, 8.*

> ⧗ *We have the best news to tell! Think of people who have not heard the good news about Jesus. How will you tell them?*

WHAT WE SHOULD DO!

📖 *Mark 1:4*

Many people think that Jesus does not matter. They may believe Jesus has come, but it does not change them.

• Why is it wrong to think like this?

John told people to 'repent' (change the way they think) because King Jesus was coming. They must hate their sins and ask Jesus to forgive them.

> ⧗ **Heaven's king has come!**
>
> • *Will you do nothing?*
>
> • *Will you leave Jesus out of your life?*
>
> • *Or will you repent and believe in Jesus?*

2 JESUS BEGINS TO TELL THE GOOD NEWS

◉ Background

Mark 1:1-15. This section is Mark's start to his book. Mark wants us to see who Jesus is (Mark 1:1, 11). He wants us to turn away from our sins and believe the good news (Mark 1:15).

◉ Main point

Jesus is God's Son. God says so. Jesus has come to tell the good news. So we should believe it and turn away from our sins ('repent').

⊡ Something to work on

Have you told the good news about Jesus many times? Perhaps it is not new to your people. Perhaps they think that they can wait until they are older. Think how to show them why Jesus' message is so important. Think of a word picture to help them. Show them why they must turn away from their sins, and believe in Jesus **today**.

⊞**Word picture example:** imagine that you are very ill. You hear that the hospital has a cure. This is very good news! So do you stay at home and die? No, you go to the hospital! The good news about Jesus is for **today**.

◉ Notes

• **Mark 1:9.** 'The Jordan' is the name of the river in which John baptised people.

• **Mark 1:10.** What is the dove? A dove is a white bird. God was showing how pleased he was with Jesus. He gave the people a picture of His Spirit coming down on Jesus. His Spirit looked like a dove.

• **Mark 1:13.** After Satan had tempted Jesus, God sent angels to look after him (Matthew 4:11).

• **Mark 1:15.** 'The time has come'. God had promised Israel a Messiah (Saviour) in the Old Testament. They have waited for many years. But now this time has come. Jesus will be the King of God's kingdom. Jesus will rule over God's people.

GOD SPEAKS!

 Mark 1:9-11

It was time for Jesus to begin his work. His work was to bring the good news.

• **What is the first thing that Jesus did (Mark 1:9)?** Jesus was 'baptised' (put under water) to be an example to us. Everyone who follows Jesus should be baptised.

• **What did God think of Jesus as Jesus began his work (Mark 1:10, 11)?** Do you remember that John told people how special Jesus was? (Mark 1:4-8) Now God speaks from heaven! John was right about Jesus. Now God says that Jesus is his Son. We must believe him.

SATAN TEMPTS!

 Mark 1:12, 13

God was pleased, but Satan (the devil) was angry. God wanted Jesus to bring the good news. Satan wanted to stop Jesus. Satan tempted Jesus to follow an easier way. ('Tempt' means to attract someone to do wrong.) But Jesus did not listen to him.

This is like God's people Israel in the desert (in Exodus and Numbers). Israel failed the test.

Israel chose not to trust God. But Jesus did not fail the test.

> ⮞ *Satan tempts us to follow an easier way. Remember Jesus. He said no to Satan. He trusted God. We can ask Jesus to help us to say no to Satan.*

JESUS PREACHES!

 Mark 1:14, 15

Jesus has passed the test. Jesus comes out of the desert to preach the good news. John cannot preach the good news any longer. (Why not? Mark 1:14). So now, Jesus tells people the same message as John did.

• **What is that message?**
 Mark 1:15.

The good news is that people do not have to wait any longer. The king has come. The person who can forgive their sins has come. It is time to do something.

> ⮞ *We do not have to wait to have our sins forgiven! Jesus has come! Praise God for Jesus. Turn away from your sins ('repent') now, and follow him. [Explain what repent means – see notes on Mark 1:1-8.]*

3 FOLLOW ME!

▣ Background

📖 *Mark 1:1-15.* **Mark** has told us that Jesus is the Christ, the Son of God. **John** has told the people that Jesus will come soon. **God** has told us that Jesus is his Son.

📖 *Mark 1:16-20.*

Now Jesus begins to **show** who he is. In Mark chapters 1-5, Jesus does many things to teach the people who he is. He shows that he has the **power to tell them what to do.** Read Mark 1:22, 27 for two examples.

In this section, Mark 1:16-20, we see the power Jesus has over some 'fishermen' (men who catch fish). These men became special followers of Jesus. We call them his **disciples**.

▣ Main point

Jesus, God's Son, has power to tell us what to do.

✦ Something to work on

Help your people to see that Jesus has power to give orders.

We do not like anyone to tell us what to do. We want to choose how we live. A real Christian is someone who does what Jesus says, like these fishermen. Think how to teach your people this. Think of a word picture to help them to understand this..

▣ Notes

• **Mark 1:16.** 'Sea of Galilee.' This is a small lake in the area of Galilee. Try to find it on a Bible map. Jesus spent most of his time in this area.

• **Mark 1:16.** 'Simon.' Later, Jesus gave him the name 'Peter'. Simon (Peter), Andrew, James and John were 4 of the 12 disciples of Jesus.

FOLLOW ME!

📖 *Mark 1:16-20*

Jesus shows that he has **power to give orders**.

⊕ **Imagine this.** You see someone who is busy at work. He has a good job. He has a house and a family to look after. You tell him to leave his work and follow you. You will not pay him money. What will he tell you to do? He will tell you to go away! But when Jesus says: 'Follow me!', what happens?

• **What did Simon and Andrew do when Jesus told them to follow him (Mark 1:18)?**

They did not argue. They did not go home to talk with their families. **Immediately**, they followed Jesus. They left their work. Now they were no longer fishermen. They were followers of Jesus.

• **What did James and John do when Jesus told them to follow him? Mark 1:20**

> ⯈ *Jesus has power to give orders. When we read the Bible, Jesus has power to tell us what to do. Jesus tells us to leave all our sin. He tells us to begin a new life of obeying him. He says 'Follow me!'*

GO FISHING FOR PEOPLE!

📖 *Mark 1:17*

Jesus had a special job for these men. Jesus does not want everyone to stop doing their usual job. He does not call everyone to be preachers.

• **What was the special job that Jesus called these fishermen to do? Mark 1:17**

Before, they caught fish. Now they must 'catch' people. Jesus will teach them to tell people the good news about him. Then some will come into his 'net', his kingdom. Jesus was calling them to become **preachers**, like him.

> ⯈ *The most important job is to tell people the good news. Jesus may not want you to leave your job. He may not call you to be a preacher. However, he does want all Christians to 'fish' for people. He does want us to help people come under Jesus' rule.*

> ⯈ *Think of people who do not understand about Jesus. Ask God to help you tell them the good news about him.*

4 JESUS TEACHES WITH POWER

▣ Background

📖 *Mark 1:16-20.* Jesus has power to **tell us what to do**. Jesus said: 'Follow me!' The fishermen left their nets and followed him.

📖 *Mark 1:29-45.* Jesus has power to **heal**.

📖 *Mark 2:1-12.* Jesus has power to **forgive sins**.

Mark has told us that Jesus is the Son of God. Now Mark shows us the power ('authority') of Jesus the Son of God.

☉ Main point

Jesus, God's Son, has power to **teach us the truth**.

✳ Something to work on

Mark does **not** mean that we can have the special powers that Jesus has. He wants us to see how special Jesus is. He wants us to see that Jesus is the Son of God. Your talk should be about Jesus. Pray that people will see how powerful Jesus is. Then they will trust Jesus. They will trust what Jesus says.

☉ NOTES

• **Mark 1:21.** 'Sabbath.' The Jews met to worship God on the Sabbath. They met in a building called a 'synagogue'. A teacher read from the Old Testament, and taught the people about God.

• **Mark 1:22.** The 'teachers of the law' often taught at the synagogue. They had studied the Old Testament ('the law') for many years.

• **Mark 1:24.** The evil spirit said Jesus' name so that he could have power over Jesus. Jesus had greater power. Jesus made the evil spirit keep quiet.

POWER TO TEACH

📖 *Mark 1:21, 22*

What made Jesus a powerful speaker?

• A loud voice?

• Lots of good stories?

No. That is not what Mark means. That is not why the people were so surprised. The people were 'amazed' (very surprised) because they knew that Jesus **spoke the truth about God**. He did not teach like the teachers of the law. Jesus did not just teach them about the Old Testament. Jesus taught them new things as well (Mark 1:27). And these new things fitted with the old things they knew.

> ⏩ *Many people teach us wrong things. They may be good speakers. Only believe them if they tell the truth about Jesus. Believe them if what they say comes from the Bible.*

> ⏩ *Jesus has power to teach. What Jesus says is true (John 14:6).*

POWER OVER EVIL SPIRITS

📖 *Mark 1:23-26*

The evil spirit was scared because he knew who Jesus was. He knew it was true that Jesus is the Son of God.

Because Jesus is the Son of God, he has power over all evil spirits. If we trust Jesus, we do not need to be afraid of evil spirits. Jesus is stronger than all evil spirits. Jesus has defeated the devil at the cross.

> ⏩ *Ask Jesus to save you from fear of evil spirits. Trust in the power of Jesus over your whole life.*

THE PEOPLE WERE VERY SURPRISED

📖 *Mark 1:27, 28*

• **What were they most surprised ('amazed') by (Mark 1:27)?**

• **What question did they ask?**

The people were not just excited because Jesus had special powers. They knew that **he was someone special**. They knew that his **teaching** had power. *[Connect this with your people.]*

5 JESUS CAME TO PREACH

◉ Background

📖 *Mark 1:21-28.* Jesus has power to **teach us the truth**.

📖 *Mark 2:1-12.* Jesus has power to **forgive sins**.

Mark is showing us the power ('*authority*') of Jesus the Son of God. In Mark 1:29-45 he gives us some more examples of Jesus' power. Mark also shows us that Jesus has not come just to do miracles.

Mark tells us three times **why** Jesus came (Mark 1:38, 2:17, 10:45).

📖 *Mark 1:29-45.*

◉ Main point

Jesus, God's Son, came to **preach**. It is more important to tell people the truth about Jesus than it is to heal them.

✴ Something to work on

This section is much longer than the other sections we have been looking at. You do not need to talk about everything in the Bible section. Use the examples of Jesus' healing to make a picture of his power. Nothing is too hard for Jesus! Jesus had all that power, and yet he did not come just to heal people. It is more important to tell people the good news.

◉ Notes

• **Mark 1:40.** 'Leprosy.' This is probably not the same disease as the leprosy we have today. The word is used for some kinds of skin disease. The Old Testament tells us about people with these skin diseases. They had to stay away from the people. They were not allowed to meet to worship God (Leviticus 13 v 45, 46). In Mark 1:44 Jesus tells the man to go to the priest so he could worship God again. It is sad that the man did not obey Jesus.

NOTHING IS TOO HARD FOR JESUS

Jesus shows that he has power over all kinds of sickness.

📖 *Mark 1:29-31.* Simon's mother-in-law.

📖 *Mark 1:32-34.* All kinds of diseases and evil spirits.

📖 *Mark 1:40-42.* Leprosy.

Here are some points to notice –

• Jesus healed people **immediately** (Mark 1:31, 42). Jesus only had to speak, or to touch someone, to heal them. This is because Jesus has God's power.

• Jesus healed people out of **love**. Notice how gentle Jesus is in Mark 1:31. Notice how he cares for the man in Mark 1:41.

• Jesus **touched** the man with leprosy, in Mark 1:41. People were afraid of leprosy. People with leprosy had to live away from everyone else. But Jesus was not afraid. His power is stronger than leprosy.

• Jesus did not want to become **famous** (Mark 1:43-45). Jesus did not want people to come to him just for his miracles. He wanted them to understand who he was.

JESUS CAME TO PREACH

📖 *Mark 1:35-39*

[Help the people to imagine what is happening.] It is early in the morning. Jesus is trying to have a quiet time on his own. Everyone is up already. They are looking for Jesus. Many people want Jesus to heal them. And what does Jesus say (Mark 1:38)?

Jesus is not being unkind. Jesus is very clear what he came to do. He did not come just to heal people. He came to tell people the good news about who he is. Jesus is not 'the healer'; he is 'the Saviour'. He must visit many towns. Everyone must hear the good news.

> ➤ *Many people today want Jesus to heal them. But Jesus did not come just to heal people. It is far more important for Jesus to save us from our sins. What good is it if Jesus heals our sickness but we still go to hell?*

6 JESUS HAS POWER TO FORGIVE SINS

◉ Background

Mark is showing us the power (*'authority'*) of Jesus the Son of God. In Mark 1:29-45 he gave us some more examples of Jesus' power.

In Mark 2:1-12 Jesus shows a different kind of power. He shows that he truly is God.

◉ Main point

Jesus has power to forgive sins. Only God can forgive sins. So Jesus is God.

⊛ Something to work on

Perhaps some of your people do not think that their sins are a big problem. They would like God to help them in many ways. However, they do not want him most of all to forgive their sins. Think how to use this story to help them. Jesus speaks in a very personal way with this man! Some people would think that Jesus was rude to talk about their sins. But Jesus knows what our biggest need is.

◉ Notes

• **Mark 2:3.** 'A paralytic.' This man was paralysed. He could not walk because his legs did not work.

• **Mark 2:4.** The houses had flat roofs. They had outside stairs so you could get onto the roof. It was easy to make a hole in the roof and it was easy to mend it again.

• **Mark 2:7.** 'Blaspheming.' This means 'speaking against God'. We 'blaspheme' if we say that we can do things that only God can do.

A SHOCKING THING TO SAY

📖 *Mark 2:1-7*

[Help the people to imagine what is happening. Tell the story so that the people feel the shock of Jesus words in Mark 2:5. What do the crowds think Jesus will say? What does the man want Jesus to say? Why are Jesus' words so shocking?]

⊕ *[Use a story to help your people.]*
Imagine a very sick boy. There is no cure for him. The family hears of a special doctor who is visiting the village. He can heal the boy. They go to him. They long to hear him say: 'Yes, I can heal him'. Instead, he says: 'You need to have your sins forgiven!' How would they feel? What would they say?

⟫ *Are these the very **best** words that you could hear Jesus say to you? Is it the most important thing in your life to have your sins forgiven?*

Some people were very shocked (Mark 2:7). In one way they were right. Only God can forgive sins. It would be very wrong for you or me to say: 'Son, your sins are forgiven'. Jesus is claiming to be God!

A WONDERFUL THING TO SAY

📖 *Mark 2:8-12*

Anyone can **say** the words 'your sins are forgiven'. How do we know if it is true? How do the people know that Jesus **can** forgive sins?

Jesus **shows** them that his words are true (Mark 2:8-12). *[Tell the story so your people can imagine what it was like. Help your people to feel the surprise of the crowds.]*

Jesus has the power to forgive sins because Jesus has the power to make the man walk. Only God has that power. **So Jesus is God.**

⟫ *'Your sins are forgiven.' These are wonderful words because Jesus has the power to say them! Jesus came to earth to forgive sins. Jesus died on the cross to forgive sins. Jesus promises to forgive our sins when we trust him. If this is the most important thing in your life, then trust Jesus today to forgive your sins.*

7 THE KIND OF PEOPLE WHO JESUS CALLS

◉ Background

In Mark 2:1-12 Jesus shows that he has the power to forgive sins. So now, Jesus shows that he did not come for good people. He came for sinners. Jesus came for people who need him to forgive their sins.

Mark 2:17 is the second time that Jesus tells us **why he came**. (See Mark 1:38.)

◉ Main point

Jesus did not come for good people. He came for sinners.

◉ Something to work on

People still think that Jesus chooses good people! Most people think that they are good people! They think that Jesus is pleased with them because they are good people. This section teaches that this is **wrong**. You need to think and pray how to say this.

You want bad people to see that Jesus came for them! You want them to ask Jesus to save them from their sin.

Some people think that they are already good. You want them to see that they are bad. You want them to ask Jesus to make them good.

◉ Notes

• **Mark 2:14.** 'Levi' is another name for **Matthew**.

• **Mark 2:14.** 'Tax collectors.' These were Jews who collected taxes for the Romans. Most people hated tax collectors, because they worked for the other side. They thought that a true Jew would never help the Romans. Most tax collectors were also cheats. They became rich because they kept too much money for themselves.

• **Mark 2:15.** 'Sinners.' We know that everyone is a sinner. But the Jews called only some people 'sinners'. These were people who lived a bad life. For example, the Jews called prostitutes 'sinners'. Tax collectors and 'sinners' were often friends. The Jews hated them all.

• **Mark 2:16.** 'Pharisees.' They were people who tried very hard to keep God's laws. They were very strict. They thought that they were good people.

JESUS CALLS SINNERS

📖 *Mark 2:17*

Are you the kind of person Jesus calls? Are you a sinner? *[Talk about the surprise of what Jesus says. Jesus came for sinners!!]*

• **This is good news for bad people!** Everyone hated all these 'sinners' and tax collectors. But Jesus came for the worst people! He loved them!

• **This is bad news for good people!** See who Jesus did **not** come to call (Mark 2:17). 'Righteous' people are good people. The Pharisees think that they are good enough already. They are not happy for Jesus to eat with bad people (Mark 2:16)!

• **This is important for saved people!** If Jesus has forgiven us, we will want to tell others about Jesus. So what kind of people will we tell? Will we only tell nice people, or people who go to church? Or will we tell bad people?

WHY JESUS CALLS SINNERS

📖 *Mark 2:17*

Jesus explains why he came for sinners. It is because they need him! *[Use Jesus' picture of a doctor to help your people understand this.]* Only sick people go to the doctor. Jesus can make all our sins better. He died on the cross to do this. Ask Jesus to forgive all your sin and make you well.

[Also, show why 'good' people do not want Doctor Jesus. They think that they are good already! They do not need him to forgive their sins.]

⊞ Tell a story about a healthy woman who visits the doctor. She tells him all about how well she is! She does not let the doctor examine her. She does not need that! She just wants him to be pleased with her! Of course, the doctor will not waste his time with healthy people! Jesus did not come for 'good' people, because they do not need a Doctor.

WHAT JESUS CALLS SINNERS TO DO

📖 *Mark 2:14*

Levi loves money. Jesus calls him away from his money. He follows Jesus. *[Show the people how this is a complete change of life for Levi.]*

Jesus calls us to leave behind our wrong way of life. He calls us to leave our sins. He calls us to turn round and follow Jesus.

⏩ *Tell a story about a person who does not take the medicine which the doctor gives her. Will she get better?*
⏩ *Will you take the medicine that Jesus gives? Will you ask him to forgive you and leave your wrong way of life?*

8 IS JESUS GOOD OR BAD?

◉ Background

Mark's Gospel is not just a collection of stories about Jesus. It is important to see this. Mark's Gospel is **one** story. It is a story that will end with the death and resurrection of Jesus.

Did you notice how the story is already moving towards the cross? At first, everyone is very surprised and pleased with Jesus. They love his teaching and healing. They think Jesus is a very good man. Then Jesus does things that some people do not like. 📖 *Mark 2:7, 16.* Now some people think that Jesus is bad! They begin to hate him. 📖 *Mark 2:18 – 3:6.* Notice how this section of the Bible ends, in **Mark 3:6.**

◉ Main point

Jesus did not come to fit in with the ways of our religion. He came to give us new life. This new life changes us inside.

◉ Notes

• **Mark 2:18.** 'Fasting.' If you 'fast' you do not eat food for a long time, often a whole day. In the Old Testament, God's people fasted at special times to show they were sorry for their sin (Leviticus 16, Exodus 34:28, Nehemiah 1:4). The Pharisees fasted often, to make God pleased with them. Probably, the disciples of John the Baptist fasted because they were sorry for their sin, and they were waiting for the Messiah to come.

• **Mark 2:19, 20.** 'Bridegroom.' Jesus uses an Old Testament picture (Hosea 2:16-20, Isaiah 54:5). God is the Bridegroom, who will marry his people. The wedding is a time for joy, not for fasting! Jesus is really saying that he is the bridegroom. His followers will be happy, not sad. It will be like a wedding.

• **Mark 2:22.** 'Wineskins.' Wine was stored in leather goat skins. The skins stretched when the wine fermented (bubbled). The skins could not stretch a second time. So new wine burst old skins.

IS JESUS BREAKING THE LAW?

📖 *Read Mark 2:18-20*

⊕ *[Use an example like this. You may think of a better example.]* In some churches people think that all good Christian men wear a tie. The Bible does not say we must wear a tie to church, but that is the church rule. They think that if a man does not wear a tie he cannot be a good Christian.

The Jews thought that all good Jews fasted. The Old Testament did not tell them to fast often, but that was their rule. Jesus was not against fasting. But he did not tell his followers to fast. So they thought that Jesus could not be a good Jew.

• Why was it the wrong time for Jesus' followers to fast? Explain this to your people. Jesus was God's Messiah. It was a time for joy, not a time to be sad.

> ⧆ *It is very easy to make the same mistake as these Jews. Do you have rules that are not in the Bible? Do you judge other Christians by your rules? A Christian life is not about rules. It is about being like Jesus.*

THE NEW WINE OF JESUS

📖 *Read Mark 2:21-22*

Jesus uses two pictures to say something very important. **Jesus did not come to fit in with the ways of our religion. Jesus came to give us new life.**

• Explain the two pictures of the cloth and the wine. Make them into stories to help the people to imagine what will happen.

The Jews had so much religion, but it was hard and stiff, like the wineskins. Our rules can be like the old wineskins. Jesus came to give us the new wine of the gospel! His truth is full of life and love. He wants to change us from the inside, not make us keep rules on the outside.

So what happens when Jesus pours his new wine into the old skins of our rules? The wineskins burst! Jesus will not let us keep the skins of religious rules.

> ⧆ *Do you want the new wine of Jesus? Do you want him to forgive you and to change you? Do you want his love to fill you so that you follow all his ways? Or do you want a religion that is like hard wineskins? You cannot have both.*

9 JESUS IS THE LORD OF THE SABBATH

◉ Background

The Jews are watching Jesus. They want to show that he really is a bad man. Will he keep all their laws?
📖 **Mark 2:18, 24 and Mark 3:2.**

The Jews were very strict about the **Sabbath**. The Sabbath is the holy day of the Old Testament.
📖 *Exodus 20:8-11.*

Mark 2:23-28 and the next section are both about the Sabbath. The Jews think that Jesus breaks the Sabbath rules.

◉ Main point

Jesus is the Lord of the Sabbath. He keeps God's laws in the right way – but do we?

⊛ Something to work on

The Pharisees ask Jesus about the **Sabbath**. But Jesus' answer is about **holy bread**. Think about this. Jesus shows them that the way they **think** is all wrong. What is wrong with the way they think about God's laws?

◉ Notes

• **Mark 2:24.** 'Pharisees.' Jews who were very strict about keeping laws. They not only kept Old Testament laws but also made many of their own laws. One of **their** laws said that you must not pick grain on the Sabbath. This was because God says that you must not work on the Sabbath. If you pick grain, you do work, because you harvest the grain! Their laws had become very silly.

• **Mark 2:25, 26.** Jesus teaches the people using the Old Testament. In Leviticus 24:5-9 God taught that only **priests** were allowed to eat the holy bread from the 'tabernacle' (God's holy place). However, in 1 Samuel 21:1-6, David and his men ate this holy bread because they were very hungry. They were not priests, but they had a great need. So God was happy for them to eat it.

• **Mark 2:28.** 'Son of Man.' Jesus often called himself 'the Son of Man'. It is a name which the Old Testament uses. It says that he is powerful as well as human.

THE SABBATH IS MADE FOR MAN!

📖 *Mark 2:27*

Sometimes it is good to break the law! Tell a story about this –

⊕ A boy is so hungry that he will die. You find him, but you have no food. In your neighbour's house there is food, but your neighbour is not there. You must not steal, so the boy dies.

Did you please God when you did not steal? No! You let the boy die. It is **right** to take the food (and give it back later!). Sometimes we need to break the law. Jesus shows this by telling the story about David. *[Tell this story.]*

God gave us his laws because they are the very best way to live. The Sabbath (and every one of God's laws) is made for man. God's laws are to help us. They are not to hurt us. God wants us to obey his laws. That is very important. But God does not only love his **laws**. He loves **us** too.

God gave us the Sabbath law to help us. *[Teach the people about the 4th Commandment.]* It is very important to have one day to rest and to think about God. God wants us to rest from our normal work, because that is good for us.

The Sabbath is made for man.

However, the Jews were like a man with a heavy bag on his back. It is so hard to walk. The bag is full of thousands of little laws that he has to keep. It is so hard to live like that. God does not want us to live like that. Jesus will never tell his disciples not to pick a few ears of grain on the Sabbath (Matthew 11:28-30)!

JESUS IS LORD OF THE SABBATH

📖 *Mark 2:28*

The Jews thought that they were lords of the Sabbath! They were the people who had the right to tell people what to do on the Sabbath!

Jesus says: 'No, you are wrong. You understand God's laws wrongly. I am Lord of the Sabbath. I understand God's law rightly. I have the right to tell people how to keep God's laws.'

> ⨠ *Do you try to keep God's laws like the Jews? You have many little rules that are like a heavy bag on your back.*
>
> *Or do you keep God's laws like Jesus? It is a joy to obey God, because you love his ways.*

10 PEOPLE WHO WANT TO KILL JESUS

▣ Background

Many Jews started to hate Jesus. Jesus said that he came for bad people! 📖 *Mark 2:17.*

Jesus did not keep to their rules! 📖 *Mark 2:18, 23.*

Jesus showed them from their own beliefs that they were wrong about their religion! 📖 *Mark 2:19-22, 25, 26.*

And Jesus even dared to say that he was Lord of the Sabbath. 📖 *Mark 2:28.*

So now the Jewish leaders look for a way to trap Jesus. They want to get him into trouble. 📖 *Mark 3:1-6.*

▣ Main point

We can be very religious but hate Jesus!

✶ Something to work on

Most people today think that Jesus was a good man. They do not hate him like these Jews. They just take no notice of him and get on with their own lives. We need to show our people that we must not do that to Jesus. If we truly understand Jesus, we will love him or hate him. We will love him for coming to be our Saviour. Or, we will hate him for showing us that we are bad people.

▣ Notes

• **Mark 3:1.** 'Shrivelled or paralysed hand.' The man's hand did not work.

• **Mark 3:2.** The Jew's rules said that you could not heal a person on the Sabbath. Jesus shows why this is wrong.

• **Mark 3:6.** 'Herodians.' These were friends of Herod and the Roman government. Usually the Pharisees hated the Herodians. Now they join to kill Jesus.

HEARTS THAT ARE HARD

 Mark 3:5

- What things in Mark 3:1-6 show that their hearts were hard and stubborn? (A 'stubborn heart' means that we will not accept the truth, we will not change.) *Think of a word picture to show what a hard heart is like.*

Tell the story to show how good and kind Jesus was, and how cruel the leaders of the Jews were. They did not care about the sick man at all! And they hated Jesus because he cared about the sick man.

Jesus asks a very easy question in Mark 3:4. We know why they did not want to answer it! It was because their hearts were hard. They did not want Jesus to do good. They only wanted Jesus to keep their rules.

> ⫸ *Is your heart growing hard? [Think of examples like the ones below.]*
>
> ⫸ *Do you **listen** to the Bible, but only **do** the things you want to? Do you tell people about Jesus, but never **help** them in life? Do you get angry when someone says that you are doing wrong?*

RELIGIOUS PEOPLE WHO KILL

 Mark 3:6

These Jews were very strict with their religion. Everyone thought that these Jews were the good people who were going to heaven. Do you think it is possible for religious people like these to hate a good man? They hated Jesus so much that they tried to murder him! In the end, these religious people killed Jesus on the cross.

Why did they want to kill Jesus? It was because he healed someone **on the Sabbath**. He broke **their** rules. We can see that there must be something very wrong with their religion!

> ⫸ *A religion that is all about rules is a very dangerous religion. It is wrong to call ourselves Christians but have a religion that is all about rules. It is wrong to be angry with Christians who do not keep our rules.*
>
> ⫸ *Do you love Jesus, or do you love your rules? Do you want to do good, or to make sure that you keep all the rules? When Jesus looks at you, is it like Mark 3:5? Ask Jesus to forgive you, and to give you a soft, loving heart.*

11 JESUS CALLS 12 DISCIPLES

▣ Background

We have seen that many Jews do not want Jesus. They should welcome Jesus as their Messiah. But they hate him because he will not keep their rules. So now Jesus turns away from them (Mark 3:7). Jesus chooses 12 people to be his special disciples. Most of the Jews do not believe, like Israel in the Old Testament. They do not want Jesus, so Jesus calls a new 'Israel' to follow him (Mark 3:13-19). Notice the number 12. There are 12 disciples like there were 12 tribes (families) of Israel.

MOST JEWS	12 DISCIPLES
very religious	Jesus' new Israel
like Israel	new family of God
do not want Jesus	follow Jesus

From now on, Jesus will take special care to teach his disciples. He does still teach the crowds, but Jesus mostly wants to teach these 12 disciples.

⊙ Main point

Jesus calls 12 disciples. Jesus chooses who **he** wants, to belong to the new family of God.

✴ Something to work on

Many people think that **we** have to choose Jesus. That is partly true. However, in the Bible Jesus always chooses us first! (John 15:16) In Mark 3, the **crowds** choose Jesus for the wrong reason. They soon go away from Jesus. But the disciples who **Jesus** chooses, stay with Jesus.

▣ Notes

- **Mark 3:12.** Jesus did not want **evil spirits** to say who he was! Even Jesus did not **say** that he was the Son of God. He wanted people to **see** it.

- **Mark 3:14.** 'Apostles.' These 12 men had a special place in Jesus' plans. They were like the foundation stones in the church. Jesus gave these men special powers (like casting out demons). We must be careful when we teach about the apostles. We must not think that we should do everything that they did.

CROWDS FOLLOW JESUS

📖 *Mark 3:7-12*

Do you follow the crowds? Do you like a popular speaker or a crowded church? That is not wrong. But to follow Jesus means **much more** than following the crowds.

Jesus was very popular. Wherever he went, the crowds followed him. They were excited about Jesus. They wanted Jesus to heal them. In Mark 3:7, Jesus left the Jews who hated him. But many ordinary Jews still crowded near Jesus.

Jesus did not want to be popular. Jesus knew that most people wanted him for the wrong reason. Soon they would leave him, because they did not like his teaching. Later they would shout: 'kill him on a cross!'

⯈ *Do you follow Jesus for the right reason? Or, do you just follow the crowd? [Talk more about the right reason to follow Jesus]*

JESUS CHOOSES 12

📖 *Mark 3:13-19*

Jesus leaves the crowds behind to choose 12 special men. Jesus knows that the crowds will soon leave him. Jesus wants men who will stay with him. He chooses them to be people who will truly believe in him. He will teach them and show them what God really wants his people to be like. Jesus does not want them to be like the Jews with all their rules. He will give them a new heart, so that they love God. *[Explain about 'old Israel' and 'new Israel' if you think that will help your people.]*

These 12 men will be 'apostles', sent by Jesus to do his work. They will belong to Jesus' new family. What kind of people will Jesus choose?

We have met some of them already. They are not very good people. They are not people who are strict with their religion. They are not clever people. They are ordinary people. Some are fishermen (James, John, Simon, and Andrew). One is a tax collector (Matthew). We will see that at first they often fail! Jesus has to teach them and change them. However, they are the people who Jesus **wants**. And they are the people who **come** when Jesus calls them (Mark 3:13).

⯈ *Jesus still calls those **he wants**. He chooses us! Not to be his apostles, but to follow him. He calls **all sorts** of people [give some examples]. Praise God if Jesus has called you because he wants you! Praise God if you have heard his call and **followed** Jesus(John 10:27, 28).*

12 THE REAL FAMILY OF JESUS

◉ Background

Many Jews hate Jesus. Jesus turns away from the old Israel and chooses disciples to belong to his new 'Israel' *Mark 3:13-19.* There are now two groups. There are people who do not believe in Jesus, and people who follow Jesus.

In Mark 3:20-35 we see who belongs to this new family of Jesus.

◉ Main point

Some people hate Jesus and refuse to believe. The new family of Jesus do what Jesus says.

◉ Something to work on

There is no middle group. Many of our people want to be in the middle. They do not want to hate Jesus, and they do not want to follow Jesus. If they are not 'for' Jesus, then they are 'against' Jesus. Help them to see that. If they do not do what Jesus says, then they cannot belong to the family of Jesus.

◉ Notes

• **Mark 3:23.** 'Parables.' Pictures or stories with another meaning. See Mark 4:1-20.

• **Mark 3:25.** 'House.' Jesus means the people in the house, the family.

• **Mark 3:28-30.** Many people are afraid that they have done the sin that cannot be forgiven. Mark 3:28 is very clear. **All** sins can be forgiven. We may have said something terrible about Jesus. God will forgive us if we ask him. The sin (or 'blasphemy') against the Holy Spirit is something different. The people in Mark 3 **refuse to see** who Jesus is. Jesus does wonderful things and they say that he has a devil! If the Holy Spirit shows us who Jesus is, and **we hate Jesus**, then we cannot be forgiven. If you love Jesus and want him to forgive you, then you have not done this sin.

THE PEOPLE WHO HATE JESUS

📖 *Mark 3:22-30*

Does it surprise you that some people hate Jesus so much? Why do people hate Jesus when he only does good things?

The Jews in Mark 3:22 are important leaders. Many people listen to them. What they say about Jesus is so unfair. Can you understand why they hate Jesus so much?

Jesus shows that what they say is stupid (Mark 3:23-27).

Of course Jesus is not working for the devil! If he were working for the devil, he would not drive out demons!

[⊕ Use the pictures that Jesus gives us to make this clear.]

Jesus warns them that what they say is serious (Mark 3:28-30).

These Jewish leaders thought they were going to heaven. They thought that they were at the top of the list! But no one who hates Jesus has God's forgiveness.

[Explain what Jesus means by the sin that will not be forgiven – see note]

THE PEOPLE WHO LOVE JESUS

📖 *Mark 3:20-21, 31-35*

Jesus' own family did not all love Jesus (Mark 3:20-21). They said that Jesus was crazy. They tried to stop Jesus from doing his work. They did not think Jesus should work so hard and care so much.

> *⊗ Do you care like Jesus? Or do you think that a **little** religion is enough? Do you think that following Jesus must not take over your life? Think carefully - do you really love Jesus?*

Jesus' true family does what Jesus says (Mark 3:31-35). Jesus does not go at once to see his brothers and mother. This is a real shock to the people! But Jesus says that his true family are the people with him. They are the people who listen to what he says. And they **do** the will of God.

> *⊗ It is possible to be like Jesus' own brothers and sisters. They want to control Jesus. They do not want to come under his word. A real Christian is someone who **obeys Jesus' teaching.** [Tell Jesus' story in Matthew 7:24-27.] Do you belong to the real family of God?*

13 LISTEN!

This is the first of two talks on this Bible section. The first talk is about why Jesus uses parables. The second talk is about the parable of the sower.

▣ Background

Already, Jesus and his teaching have divided people into two groups:

• people who turn away from Jesus

• people who believe in Jesus

From now on, Jesus spends most of his time with the second group. He teaches his disciples and the people who will listen to him.

Jesus' **parables** also divided the crowds into two groups.
📖 *Mark 4:1-20.*

⊙ Main point

'He who has ears to hear, let him hear' (Mark 4:9).

(When you teach the Bible, look out for verses like Mark 4:9, which are like a key to unlock the teaching. This parable is about how we listen to God's word. So at the end of his parable, Jesus tells us to be very careful how we listen.)

✦ Something to work on

Listen carefully to what Jesus says in Mark 4:11, 12. (We explain this on the next page.) It may sound hard to us. We must not shut out what Jesus says. We must not change Jesus' words to make them say what we want. If God has made you a teacher, you must teach what the Bible says.

⊙ Notes

• **Mark 4:2.** 'Parables.' Stories which teach about God and God's kingdom. Often people were not ready to hear the truth in a direct way. So Jesus told parables to make people think. Often Jesus' parables showed up their sin. Jesus' parables divided people into two groups. People who wanted to listen and people who did not. A parable is like a sieve, or a filter. It separates what is good from what is bad.

TO PEOPLE WHO WILL LISTEN

📖 *Mark 4:1-3,9*

There was a large crowd of people listening to Jesus. They did not all have the right kind of ears!

• What kind of ears does Jesus want us to have?

> 🔊 *We can be in the crowds that come to church. We can listen to the Bible and the talk. We can even say that it was a good talk.* **But we only have good ears when God's word goes into our lives and changes us.**

The crowds knew that Jesus' story about the soils was about them. In Mark 4:9 Jesus is saying: 'So what will you do about it?' The story tells the truth about them. Will they take notice? Will **we** take notice?

⊕ *[This is very important. Find a picture to help the people. This one may help.]* You watch a football match. You enjoy the match. You cheer when your team scores a goal. You talk about the match afterwards. But the match does not change you! You come to church. You enjoy the meeting. You sing the songs. You even talk about church. **But does it change you?** Or is it just like when you watch a football match?

TO PEOPLE WHO WILL NOT LISTEN

📖 *Mark 4:10-12*

Notice what happened when Jesus finished his story. The story made them think. They knew Jesus spoke about them. Yet only a few people stayed to ask Jesus about his story.

Jesus explains his story. But first he explains why he teaches with **parables**. It is to find out the people who want to know the truth (Mark 4:11, 12).

What Jesus says may surprise us. Jesus uses parables **to keep people out!** Jesus knew his story would turn people away, but he did not mind that! In fact, Jesus wants to make sure that these people stay outside! He does not want people to follow him for the wrong reasons. Jesus tells us here that he tells parables to **judge** people. What do we learn from this?

Jesus is **not** judging people who do not know about him. These people are **Jews**. They should have welcomed Jesus, their Messiah. But they had hard hearts. They refuse to listen to Jesus. So Jesus **judges** them. He does not teach them in a direct way. Instead He tells parables which they will not understand well. Just as the prophet Isaiah had said (Mark 4:12).

> 🔊 *Jesus' words either change us or judge us. What about you?*

14 PARABLE OF THE SOWER

◉ Background

Jesus' **parables** split the crowds into two groups. Jesus is happy for most of the crowd to go away after the story. A few stay to find out what the parable really means.

📖 Mark 4:10

Remember, Jesus wants to teach his disciples. One thing he teaches them is how to sow. This parable has lessons for **soils** and lessons for **sowers**.

◉ Main point

God's word only saves some people who hear it. But those people give a big harvest.

✳ Something to work on

Everyone likes to think that they are 'good soil'. We need to help people to see that what matters is **a crop**. We can love to hear God's message, but that is no good to the farmer. He only looks for crops at harvest time.

What are those crops? What does God look for in our lives, which show that his word has changed us? What pleases him?

◉ Notes

• **Mark 4:3.** 'Sower' or farmer This farmer sowed his seed in his fields. He scattered seed with his hand as he walked.

A MESSAGE FOR THE SOILS

📖 *Mark 4:14-20*

⊕ Imagine four different people who are like the four soils. Talk about what happens when they hear God's word. Help the people to see who they are most like. After the talk, the people could get into groups to think more about the soils.

• **The path** (Mark 4:4, 15). The devil is like a bird looking for seed. He hates God's word to go deep into our lives. He wants us to forget very quickly.

• **The stony soil** (Mark 4:5-6, 16-17). These people are very happy to hear the Bible. They put up their hands and say that they want to be Christians. But what happens when it becomes difficult? Why?

• **The thorns (weeds)** (Mark 4:7, 18-19). These people also start to grow. God's word begins to change them. But they are more interested in the things of this life. They do not pull up the 'weeds'. What are these weeds?

• **The good soil** (Mark 4:8, 20). Are you saying: 'Lord, make me like this! I want God to have a big harvest in my life. I want to bring God praise. I want to help others come to know Jesus.'

➡ *We all hear good seed! Does that seed change your life? Does it make you turn from your sin and trust in Jesus? Does it make you love and obey him? The only soil that pleases God is the one that gives him* **crops**.

A MESSAGE FOR SOWERS

📖 *Mark 4:11*

Jesus told this story to his **disciples**. They must learn to be people who sow God's word. When God teaches us these things, we must tell them to others! We become sowers. Sowers must learn two things.

1. Only a few will be saved. In the end, only one soil gave any crops to the farmer. Many people will hear. Sometimes, many people will say they are Christians. It makes us sad when only a few grow to be like Jesus. Only a few are really saved. Jesus tells us to **expect** this.

2. There will be a big harvest (Mark 4:20). We must not be too sad! Only one soil gave any crops. However, that soil gave a **big** crop! Only one person may become a true Christian, but that person will bring a lot of praise to God. When we sow God's seed, it is hard work. It can be very disappointing. But never give up. In the end, there **will be** a big harvest.

📖 *Galatians 6:9.*

15 SHARE GOD'S TRUTH!

▣ Background

Jesus has just told the parable of the sower. It is a parable about the teaching of Jesus. The other parables in Mark 4 follow on from the parable of the sower. There are two more seed parables (Mark 4:26-32). They also teach about the way that we hear Jesus' words.

The two parables in Mark 4:21-25 are also about how we hear Jesus' words. If we are good soil, what do we do with Jesus' words next? We must share God's word with other people.

⊙ Main point

We must share God's word with other people.

✦ Something to work on

It is hard to work out **exactly** what Jesus means in these two parables. Read Mark 4:1-34 many times and pray to understand. How do the parables in Mark 4:21-25 fit in?

In your talk, make sure that the **main point** is very clear. It is a very important message. We do not want to confuse people.

▣ Notes

• **Mark 4:22.** We do not hide something forever. The reason to hide something is to keep it safe for the right time. Then we will let people see what we hid! God 'hid' the good news about Jesus for a long time. He gave us clues in the Old Testament. But now it is time to bring out the message for everyone to hear!

• **Mark 4:24.** 'With the measure you use, it will be measured to you – and even more' (NIV). GNB translates it like this: 'The same rules you use to judge others will be used by God to judge you.' The first translation is better. The word Jesus uses is a 'measure', like a spoon or a jug. I think Jesus is talking about how we share his words. Do we use a small spoon or a big bucket to give out God's words? He wants us to be generous when we share his words. And he will be generous to us.

BE A LAMP!

📖 *Mark 4:21-23*

⊕ Tell a story or act it out. It is dark. One person has a lamp or torch. But he does not want to share it with the other people. He wants to keep all the light for himself. So he hides the light under a blanket or mat! Now nobody has any light! How silly!

Jesus, the Light of the world, has come. Without Jesus, everyone is in the dark. Did Jesus keep the truth to himself? Of course not! The light must shine. The truth must come out. God's word must be shared. So Jesus taught God's truth.

Do you have the light of Jesus? Imagine a Christian who does not want to share his light. Perhaps he is scared what others will think. So he tries very hard not to let any light out. How does he do that? How do **you** do that sometimes?

> ➢ *Jesus called John the Baptist a 'bright and shining light'. Is that true for you? Will you pray that it will be true? Who do you want to share God's truth with this week?*

BE A BUCKET!

📖 *Mark 4:24-25*

⊕ Imagine a rich man or woman with a big lake of pure water. No one else has any water, because there has been no rain. Everyone comes to this person and asks for some water. Will he measure out a little water in a cup? Or will he give a big bucket or can?

> ➢ *Jesus says: 'Be generous! Give lots!' These parables are about how we hear God's word. When we hear God's word, we must give it away again! We are like someone with a big lake of water. Everyone is thirsty. They need to know God's truth. Will you keep it all to yourself? Will you only share a little bit in a cup? Or will you be like a big bucket. Will you share lots of God's word?*

Then what happens? 📖 Mark 4:25. The more we have, the more we get. If we put God's word into practice, we become strong. If we give it away to other people, we become rich. Think of Christians you know. Jesus' words are so true! And what happens to people who hear God's word and do nothing with it? They go away from God. In the end, they lose everything.

16 SEED GROWS!

▣ Background

Jesus tells two more parables about seeds. Remember that he wants to teach his **disciples**. Jesus wants them to become teachers like him. He wants them to understand how the seed of God's word grows. Jesus does not want the disciples to give up when nothing happens. So he tells them two stories to help them.

📖 Mark 4:26-34

⊙ Main point

Trust God's word to grow.

✳ Something to work on

We must make the parables talk to our people. Tell stories which are like Jesus' parables. Tell stories which are like real life to them. Can your people remember the time they went away, came back, and found that something (or someone!) had grown tall? Do your people know a tiny seed like the mustard seed, which grows into a tree? Or other things which began very small, and became very big? Use the things that they know.

▣ Notes

• **Mark 4:26,30.** 'The kingdom of God is like…' Jesus means 'let me tell you something about the kingdom of God.' Jesus often used these words to begin his parables. Jesus' parables show how different God's kingdom is from the world. The 'kingdom of God' is where God rules. We belong to the kingdom of God if Jesus is our King.

• **Mark 4:26-29.** Jesus does not mean that there is **nothing** for the farmer to do, after he has sown the seed. Jesus does not mean there is **nothing** for a Christian to do, after he has taught God's word. We must pray. Often we must tell more of God's word. But the point is that **we** cannot make the seed grow.

IT GROWS ON ITS OWN!

📖 *Mark 4:26-29*

I have heard of people who talk to their plants to make them grow! How silly!

⊞ Imagine a farmer who cannot get to sleep because he is worried about his seeds. It is cold. There is no sun. So he gets out of bed to help his seeds to grow... How silly! The farmer just needs to wait. The seed will grow without any help. God gives the sun and the rain, and the plant grows.

Praise God for that miracle! Every year, little seeds grow into crops for us to eat. A seed looks too small to do anything! But in that seed is life. In the seed is everything that it needs to grow into a big plant.

Jesus says that it is like that with **his words**. They seem very small. They do not seem important or powerful. **But they have life**. God's words grow in our lives. They grow into crops.

> ⧉ *Trust God's word to grow. When you teach God's word, do not worry about the seed. It has a life of its own. God, not you, makes it grow. Just keep on sowing God's word. Then, one day, you will see how the seed has grown.*
> ***See Isaiah 55:10, 11.***

IT GROWS BIG!

📖 *Mark 4:30-32*

[Tell the story. Something that is so small grows so big! What a surprise! A seed that the birds might eat grows into a tree that the birds sit in!]

It is like that with God's words. Maybe you tell people about Jesus and the cross, and they have no interest. You go home and feel sad. You think that it is no use. The seed seems too weak and it will not change anyone. However, someone has listened. The seed grows. All his sins are forgiven. All his life changes. He tells many people about Jesus. He has eternal life. God's word has become a big tree!

> ⧉ *Trust God's word to grow. Do not decide that it has done nothing, when it **seems** like that. We may not see much happen, but remember that tiny things can grow very big.*
>
> *Trust God's word to grow. Do not try to **change** the seed because it looks so small! Do not make it look bigger or better to attract people! Trust the message about God and sin, Jesus and his cross.*

17 WHO IS THIS?

⊡ Background

So far in Mark…

- Jesus has come to preach the good news about God's kingdom.
- Jesus has shown his power over people, disease, and sin.
- Many Jews hate Jesus and want to kill him.
- Jesus has left these people and called disciples to be the 'new Israel'.
- Jesus has taught in parables, to help the disciples understand about his kingdom.

However, the disciples still do not understand who Jesus really is…

This is the big question of Mark 1-8. Mark wants us to answer their question: **'Who is this?'**

⊡ Main point

The winds and waves obey Jesus. We should put our faith in him.

⊠ Something to work on

Fear or faith? Some people think that they do not need to trust Jesus or be afraid of his power. Be careful to show that we have to take Jesus' power seriously. If we do not trust him to save us, we should be very afraid.

⊡ Notes

• **Mark 4:39:** Usually, waves take hours to go calm after the wind stops. This miracle shows Jesus' great power.

WHO IS THIS?

📖 *Mark 4:35-41*

First, Jesus does not seem to care. He is asleep, while the boat sinks! He is their Teacher, but he does nothing to help his disciples!

> ›› *Do you feel like that, sometimes? You are in trouble. Jesus did not help you. He let you get into trouble. You know that he has power to do something. But Jesus seems to be asleep! It feels as if he does not care. **Never believe that!** (Isaiah 43:1-3)*

Then, **Jesus shows who he is.**

⊕ Imagine that you are in a boat. A storm comes. You tell everyone 'don't worry, I will stop it!' You shout 'Stop, wind! Be still, waves!' What happens next? Nothing. Your friends think that you are crazy. They are right!

• So why can Jesus talk to the wind and waves like this? Why do they obey Jesus immediately? Who is this? Who alone could have such power?

['Who is this?' You may decide not to answer that question. Your people may need to work it out for themselves. The disciples do not know the answer yet. We know that only the God who made the sea can do this. But the disciples do not see yet that Jesus is God.]

FEAR OR FAITH?

📖 *Mark 4:40*

The disciples were afraid when Jesus did nothing. Now they are afraid when he makes the sea go calm! There is no wind, no waves. Jesus has saved them. Yet, they are even more afraid!

They are afraid of Jesus' power, because they do not know **who Jesus is**.

They should have seen that Jesus is their **God** and **Saviour!** He saved them from the sea! They have nothing to fear!

> ›› *Jesus is **God**. He has all power over us. He can do what he likes to us. One day he will be our Judge. Are you afraid of him?*
>
> ›› *Jesus is **Saviour**. If you will trust him, you do not need to be afraid of his power. Jesus came to save us from our sins.*
> 📖 *John 3:16-18, 31*
>
> ›› *Then his power is **for us**, not against us. Then it does not matter how big the storm is, because Jesus will look after us.*

49

18 JESUS HAS POWER OVER DEMONS

▣ Background

The big question in Mark 1-8 is: 'Who is Jesus?' Now we have reached Mark 5, we know that Jesus has power to:

- heal the sick (even people with leprosy) and cast out demons.

- forgive sin.

- teach with God's power and call disciples.

- tell the sea to obey him.

However, the disciples still ask the question 'Who is this?' (Mark 4:41). They still do not trust Jesus to be the Son of God. In Mark 5, Jesus again shows who he is. Will the people believe – or be afraid of his power?
📖 *Mark 5:1-43.*

☉ Main point

Jesus has power over demons. We should put our faith in him and tell everyone what he has done for us!

✱ Something to work on

If you look at our notes on Mark 4:35-41, you will see that we have given you the same talk headings! The stories are different, but they teach the same important things about Jesus. Ask God to show your people these big lessons. They need to see who Jesus really is, and trust him completely.

▣ Notes

- **Mark 5:1.** See a Bible map if you have one. This area was the side of the lake where mostly Gentiles (not Jews) lived.

- **Mark 5:13.** Do not feel sorry for the pigs! We know that Jesus is not cruel. We know that Jesus is fair. The important thing is the harm these demons did to the **man**. Jesus set him free from demons who wanted to take him to hell.

- **Mark 5:20.** 'Decapolis' is an area of 10 cities. Notice how the man told many more people than Jesus said!

WHO IS THIS?

📖 *Mark 5:1-13*

[Use Mark 5:3-5 to describe this man. His terrible strength, his many devils, his own great pain. Everyone is afraid of him.]

• So what does Jesus do when this frightening man runs towards him?
Why does Jesus not run away?
Who is afraid in Mark 5:6-10?

The reason that this man is afraid of Jesus is that he **knows who Jesus is** (Mark 5:7). The disciples are still blind, but the devils in this man see! (James 2:19) The man is so afraid, but he has to bow down to the Son of God. The devils in the man know that Jesus has power to do to them what he wants. They can only ask for mercy.

> ⟫ *If we know the Son of God, **we never need to be afraid of evil spirits**! The evil spirits are afraid of Jesus, because Jesus has power over them.*

> ⟫ *Are you still afraid of evil spirits? Remember that Jesus will judge them. Trust Jesus, the Son of God, and do not be afraid.*

FEAR OR FAITH?

📖 *Mark 5:14-20*

How strange! 📖 *Mark 5:15, 17.* The man is now at peace, but the people are afraid! Jesus has saved them from this frightening man, but they want Jesus to go away!

Why is this? Because they are afraid of Jesus' power. They are afraid of what Jesus might do to them.

> ⟫ *Are you afraid of Jesus' power? Are you afraid to follow Jesus, because you know that he has power over you? Maybe you do not want him to have power over you. Think carefully. Jesus is the only Saviour. It is very wrong to want Jesus to go away.*

Now the man was so different! He had **faith**. 📖 *Mark 5:18-20.* He trusted Jesus because Jesus had set him free. He wanted to be with Jesus.

But see that Jesus had a job for him to do. He did not only tell his **family**. He told everyone he could find about **how much** Jesus had done for him.

> ⟫ *How much has Jesus done for you?*
> *How much will you tell others?*

19 LESSONS ABOUT FAITH

⊡ Background

So far in Mark, we have not seen much faith in Jesus. Jesus has to question why the disciples do not trust him. 📖 *Mark 4:40.*

Now Mark shows us two people who come to Jesus with faith. They trust Jesus' love and power to help them. 📖 *Mark 5:21-43* – and see how Mark puts the two stories together. He does this because both stories teach the same lesson.

We have divided the section into two talks, because there is so much to learn.

⊡ Main point

Have faith in Jesus, like Jairus and the woman.

⊡ Something to work on

The stories tell us about faith in Jesus. These people trusted Jesus to help them in their need. We need Jesus too. We need Jesus, most of all, to save us from our sin. These stories help us to see how to trust Jesus to save us from our sin. Pray that your people will see that this is their biggest need. Help them to see that it is very safe to trust in Jesus.

⊡ Notes

• **Mark 5:22.** Jarius is an important Jew. He teaches people in the synagogue. See how different he is from other Jewish leaders who we have read about!

• **Mark 5:25.** The bleeding makes the woman '**unclean**' by Old Testament laws. This means that she cannot go to worship God with other people. She feels separated from everyone. She is afraid of what people think of her.

FAITH IN JESUS IS HUMBLE

📖 *Mark 5:22*

Jairus was a very important man. But he knows that Jesus is far more important! So he bows before Jesus.

> ➔ *If we have true faith in Jesus, we will be very humble. We will not think how good we are. We will think how good Jesus is. We will come and worship Jesus, and ask him to show mercy to us.*

FAITH IN JESUS COMES FROM A GREAT NEED

📖 *Mark 5:23, 25-26*

These people trusted in Jesus because they needed to! *[Describe their great need. Show that what they needed was not a small thing. It was the most important thing in their life.]*

> ➔ *We can ask Jesus to help us with small things, but Jesus came to help us with our **biggest need**. We have sin that is killing us. We are in danger of hell. Go to Jesus with your biggest need. Ask Jesus to save you.*

FAITH IS IN JESUS ONLY

These two people knew that nothing else could help them. The woman had tried many doctors. Jairus knew that his daughter was nearly dead. Jesus was their only hope.

> ➔ *Is Jesus your only hope? Jesus is the one person in the world who has power to make you clean from your sin. Only Jesus can save you from death and hell. Do not trust anything else. Go to Jesus only.*

FAITH IN JESUS DOES NOT MAKE US ASHAMED

Imagine Mark 5:21, 22. Suddenly someone pushes through the crowd. He is not polite, he does not care what people think. This man needs Jesus, now!

Imagine Mark 5:33. The woman is afraid at first. She knows how cruel people are to an 'unclean' woman. But now she trusts Jesus. She is not ashamed to say what he has done for her.

> ➔ *If you have faith in Jesus, you will not be ashamed. Perhaps you are like the woman. You want to be secret. You want just to reach out to Jesus and hope that no one sees. But Jesus does not want us to be ashamed of him.*

20 MORE LESSONS ABOUT FAITH

▣ Background

See the **BACKGROUND** for the last talk.

Remember how Mark has shown us the power of Jesus. Jesus has control over disease, evil spirits, sin, the sea, everything!

Notice Jesus' power again in Mark 5. See how calm Jesus is. See how he stops to talk to the woman, when he is on the way to a dying girl. See how the woman only needs to touch Jesus' clothes to heal her. See how Jesus talks to a dead girl and makes her completely better.

⊙ Main point

Have faith in Jesus, like Jairus and the woman.

✖ Something to work on

We have given you some lessons about faith. These lessons come from the story about Jairus. Try to make the story come to life as you teach the lessons. Help your people to imagine how Jairus feels.

▣ Notes

* **Mark 5:39.** Jesus says that the girl is 'asleep'. Everyone knows that she is dead. Jesus knows that she is dead. However, Jesus means that it is not a problem for him. Jesus has such power that he can 'wake up' a dead person.
  📖 **John 11:11-14.**

* **Mark 5:43.** Jesus often told people to be quiet about his miracles. Jesus did not want the crowds to get excited about miracles. He wanted the miracles to **show who he is**. This is important for us today. Miracles are not the main thing. People need to **know** Jesus, more than they need him to heal them. They need to trust Jesus, the Son of God, the only Saviour.

FAITH IN JESUS HELPS US TO WAIT

Imagine that you are Jairus. Your daughter is dying. Jesus is coming, but he is so slow. Then he stops to speak to a woman. Oh no! Then you hear the bad news. 'Your daughter is dead.'

Jairus had to wait. How did that help him? Waiting **feels** like a bad thing, but really it is good. Jesus makes Jairus' faith stronger.

> ⏩ *We do not like to wait - but we must trust Jesus. He sometimes seems so slow to come and help you - but you need to trust Jesus. Things may have got worse for you - but you must trust Jesus.*

FAITH IN JESUS IS STRONGER THAN FEAR

📖 *Mark 5:35,36*

'Your daughter is dead!' It looks as if Jesus is too late. But what does Jesus say?

> ⏩ *[Ask your people to think about their fears.] What does Jesus say to us (Mark 5:36)?*

FAITH IN JESUS MEANS THAT WE BELIEVE WHAT HE SAYS

📖 *Mark 5:36*

Jairus hears two things. 'Your daughter is dead' and 'Do not be afraid'. Is it safe for him to trust Jesus' words? Of course! It is not easy, but Jesus never lies.

> ⏩ *When do you find it hard to trust Jesus' words? Will you trust what you feel like, or what Jesus says? Which one is safe? [⊞ Find a word picture to help. For example, Jesus' words are like a big rock. The waves of the sea crash around you, but it is always safe to stand on the big rock.]*

FAITH IN JESUS WILL NEVER DISAPPOINT YOU

📖 *Mark 5:42*

Remember that this girl is dead. Her body is cold. Yet Jairus still trusts Jesus to raise her from the dead! Was he disappointed? Immediately the girl is full of life, and ready to eat a good meal!

> ⏩ *Nothing is too hard for Jesus. We can trust him with impossible things. If Jesus has promised, he will not disappoint us.*
> 📖 *1 John 5 v 14, 15.*

21 JESUS' HOME TOWN

◉ Background

Mark 5 showed us three people who had faith in Jesus. However, most people will not believe in Jesus. They want his miracles, but they will not believe that Jesus has come from God to save them.

In Mark 6, we see that the people in Jesus' own town do not want him. Mark has shown us this before. 📖 *Mark 3:20, 21, 31-35.*

Luke tells us more about Jesus' visit to Nazareth. Luke tells us that, in the end, they try to throw Jesus off a cliff. 📖 *Luke 4:16-30.*

◉ Main point

These people, who know Jesus well, do not want him.

✶ Something to work on

How might we be like the people of Nazareth? Our people probably will not say bad things about Jesus. But they may have the same lack of faith. They may know so much about Jesus, but still push Jesus away. They may not want Jesus to be Lord over them. They may not trust Jesus to be their Saviour.

Pray that God will give your people faith as you teach them.

◉ Notes

• **Mark 6:1.** Jesus' home town was Nazareth, where he grew up.

• **Mark 6:5, 6.** Jesus 'could not do miracles' there because of their 'lack of faith'. Jesus did miracles to help people believe in him. If they would not believe, then Jesus would not do miracles.

• **Mark 6:6.** Jesus was 'amazed' or 'surprised'. Jesus is fully God, but he is also fully human. As a human on earth, he did not know everything. He is surprised here by Nazareth. These people know so much about Jesus, and still they do not believe. Jesus is surprised that their hearts are so hard.

PEOPLE WHO KNOW SO MUCH ABOUT JESUS

📖 *Mark 6:2-3*

What do they know about Jesus?

- Jesus' **teaching** and **wisdom** surprises them.

- They know about his **miracles**.

- They have been with him as he grew up as a '**carpenter**' (person who makes things out of wood).

They do not find anything bad about Jesus. It is all good. Everything they know about Jesus is good. Yet still they will not accept him (Mark 6:3).

> ⟫ *What do you know about Jesus? Is it all good?*
> *Is there anything about Jesus that makes you afraid to trust him? If not, why will you not accept him?*
>
> *The more we know about Jesus, the more we should believe in him. [Tell your people many reasons to believe in Jesus.] We know so many good things about Jesus. Why will you not trust in him?*

PEOPLE WHO WILL NOT BELIEVE IN JESUS

📖 *Mark 6:3, 6*

Mark tells us why these people did not believe in Jesus. **They did not want to!** They knew Jesus! They hated to think that Jesus was better than they were. They did not want the carpenter to tell them how to live!

They could **see** that Jesus was very special. But they did not love him and believe in him. Instead, they hated him.

> ⟫ *Are you like these people? You believe everything about Jesus, but you do not want him to be your Lord? Why is that?*
>
> *Do you need to ask Jesus to forgive your surprising lack of faith?*

Are you shocked when people know so much about Jesus, but do not want him? The reason is that they do not want Jesus the carpenter to tell them how to live. They do not want Jesus to be their King.

22 TELL EVERYONE ABOUT JESUS!

▣ Background

Mark 6:1-29 tells us what happens when people do not want the message of Jesus.

- **Mark 6:1-6** tells us happened to **Jesus** in his home town.

- **Mark 6:14-29** tells us what happened to **John the Baptist**, when he told Herod to repent.

- In the middle is **Mark 6:6-13**. This shows what may happen to the **12 disciples**, when they tell people to repent and believe in Jesus.

▣ Main point

We need to tell everyone the good news about Jesus. But do not expect everyone to like it!

▣ Something to work on

Some things in this section are important for us today. Other things were just for the 12 disciples then. How can we tell which things are for us today? It helps to remember that our mission (job) is **different** and **the same**!

- One reason that it is **different** is that the disciples spoke to **Jews**. They told the people to repent because their King had come. The people should welcome the disciples because they brought this good news. For us, many people who we speak to do not know very much. We need to be patient.

- It is the **same** because Jesus told his church to go into the world and preach the good news. Everyone needs to know about Jesus. When we tell people about Jesus, we do need to trust Jesus to be with us. But we do not need to go without food or money.

▣ Notes

- **Mark 6:7.** Jesus gave them power over evil spirits to prove that they told the truth about Jesus. It is different for us because we have the Bible. We can show people what **God says** about Jesus.

- **Mark 6:11.** Jews used to shake off the dust when they came out of a non-Jewish town. It showed what they thought of non-Jews. But here it shows what **God** thinks of **Jews** who will not believe the good news about Jesus. God wants to show them that they are not his people any more.

TELL EVERYONE ABOUT JESUS!

 *Mark 6:7,12*

- **Mark 6:6:** Jesus goes to the villages.

- **Mark 6:7:** Jesus sends his **disciples** to the villages.

Jesus shows his disciples what to do, and then he sends them to do it! Like Jesus, they had power to heal and cast out evil spirits. Everyone must know that Jesus is the Saviour from God. The people must repent (turn from their sins) and believe in Jesus.

Jesus' main work is to die for our sins and rise again. The work that Jesus gives to **us** (his disciples) is to tell everyone about Jesus.

All the Jews needed to know that their Saviour had come. Everyone in the world needs to know that the Saviour has come.

> ⟫ *Does everyone in your town or village know about Jesus? Does everyone in the villages near you know about Jesus? Do they know the **truth** about Jesus?*
>
> ⟫ *They need to know about Jesus! Who are the best people to tell them? Matthew 28:18-20*

DO NOT EXPECT EVERYONE TO LIKE THE GOOD NEWS!

 Mark 6:11

Do not think that it is easy to tell people about Jesus.

If people will not even welcome **Jesus**, then they will not always welcome Jesus' **disciples**! Many people do not want to repent of their sin and believe in Jesus. They may tell us to go away or they may hurt us.

- So should we change the message to make it easier?

- Should we stop telling people about Jesus because they do not want to know?

No! Remember that people came to **our** town or village to tell people about Jesus. It was not easy, but they did not give up. So, today, we know about Jesus. *[Tell a true story about this.]*

In Mark 6:11 Jesus tells the disciples to leave any villages that do not want him. It is always very wrong to say no to Jesus. But the people who we speak to are different from these Jews. They do not know what is true. We must be patient. We must be ready for them to hurt us.

23 HEROD AND JOHN THE BAPTIST

◉ Background

Mark 6:1-29 tells us what happens when people do not want the message of Jesus.

• **Mark 6:1-6** tells us what happened to **Jesus** in his home town.

• **Mark 6:6-13** tells us what may happen to the **12 disciples** when they tell people to repent and believe in Jesus.

• **Mark 6:14-29.** tells us what happened to **John the Baptist**, when he told Herod to repent. It is also about what happened to **Herod**, after he refused to repent.

◉ Main point

Be ready to suffer. Be like John the Baptist!

Be quick to repent. Do not be like Herod!

✦ Something to work on

Many people may not know this story about Herod. Think how you can help them to understand it. You could ask different people to read the Bible verses for John, Herod, Herodias and Herodias' daughter. Before they read, you could talk about what kind of person each one is.

◉ Notes

• **Mark 6:16:** Herod was afraid! He knew that he had done wrong. Also, why did Herod not know that **Jesus** did the miracles? We can be sure that John told him about Jesus. When we turn away from Jesus, we become blind to the truth. Follow Herod's story (Luke 23:8-12; Acts 12:23).

• **Mark 6:17.** This long story about John the Baptist happened months before. Mark puts in this story because it is another example of a faithful preacher. It is not easy to tell people to repent!

WE MUST NOT CHANGE THE MESSAGE!

📖 *Mark 6:17-18*

⊕ Tell a true story about a Christian who died for Jesus. Why did the Christian die? It was because he told the truth! He did not change the message to save his life!

John the Baptist died because he told the truth. *[Tell the story. Imagine how hard it was to tell King Herod that he did wrong! (Mark 6:18) Imagine John in prison. He longs to get out! He knows that Herod will call him again soon. If John says nice things, maybe Herod will let him go!]*

But John will not change the message. He tells Herod that he is wrong and that he must repent. In the end, that is why Herod cuts off John's head.

» *Does this story make you feel afraid? Or does it help you to be strong?*

If we change the message, people will not hurt us. But also, they will not hear the truth about Jesus. And Jesus will not be pleased with us. Matthew 5:10-12.

THE MESSAGE MUST CHANGE US!

1. Herod liked to listen, but he did not want to change!
📖 *Mark 6:20*

We can be sure that John told Herod many things about Jesus. Herod liked to hear these things. But he did not want to give up Herodias, his brother's wife. He did not want to believe in Jesus, because he did not want to change.

» *Are you like that? You like to hear about Jesus. You come to church. But what sin do you love? What keeps you from following Jesus?*

2. Herod liked John, but he still killed him! 📖 *Mark 6:27*

Why did Herod kill John? If Herod had listened to John's message, would he have killed John? What happens when we choose our sin instead of Jesus?

Herod's heart became so hard that he killed God's prophet!

Do you know people who said that they believed in Jesus? Years ago, they came to church, but they did not want to leave their sin. Do they love Jesus now? Do they listen to God's word now?

Do not be like Herod!

24 JESUS FEEDS FIVE THOUSAND SHEEP!

▣ Background

Mark 6:1-29 tells us what happens when people do not want the message of Jesus.

Now the disciples have come back from their preaching trip.
📖 *Mark 6:7, 30.*

It looks like the trip was very successful. Many people want to see Jesus. Jesus and the disciples try to find a quiet place to rest. But thousands of people run miles round the lake to find Jesus.
📖 *Mark 6:30-33.*

What do they want? Do they want the **message** of Jesus? Or do they just want the **miracles**?

▣ Main point

Jesus is not just a miracle-maker. He came to meet our real needs.

▣ Something to work on

This section is hard to teach, because Jesus speaks by his **actions** as well as by his words. The miracle **means** something (Mark 6:52).

Study John 6 carefully to understand this miracle better.

Talk more about Jesus than about the loaves and fish, because this miracle is about who Jesus is.

▣ Notes

• Matthew, Mark, Luke and John all tell about this miracle. This shows how important it is.

• **Mark 6:31.** The disciples needed some rest. However, the crowds had greater needs...

• **Mark 6:34.** A shepherd is a farmer who looks after sheep. A shepherd leads the sheep so that they do not get lost.

• **Mark 6:37.** Jesus has many lessons to teach his **disciples**. He wants them to see that only he can feed this big crowd. Will they trust Jesus better after this miracle?

Read on! 📖 *Mark 6:45-52.*

WHAT DO WE NEED?

📖 *Mark 6:34*

- By the end of the day, the people **need food**! There is no way to get enough food. So Jesus does this wonderful miracle.

- However, the people **need much more than food**. What does Jesus see when he looks at this crowd of people? 📖 *Mark 6:34.*

They are like lost sheep. They do not know where to go in life. They have no Shepherd to tell them the true way to follow. They follow each other. They follow the latest exciting thing. And the latest exciting thing is an astonishing man who does miracles.

What do they need? They need to know who Jesus really is. They need to know that Jesus is 'the Way, the Truth and the Life' (John 14:6). They need to know that Jesus is the Good Shepherd, who will give his life for the sheep.

> ⏩ *Are you like those people? Do you follow the crowd? Do you follow the latest exciting teaching? Do you want miracles?* ***You need to know the real Jesus.*** *[Talk about Jesus, the Saviour of sinners, and the Lord over our lives.]*

WHAT DOES JESUS GIVE?

Jesus does not just give them what they **want**. He gives them what they **need**.

- Jesus gives them **food**. He cares that they are hungry!
- Jesus gives them **teaching**. 📖 *Mark 6:34.* They need to hear the truth.
- Jesus gives them a **special** miracle. This miracle is not just to fill their stomachs. It is not just to make them excited. It is to make them see **who Jesus is**. It is a **sign** to teach them. It is like a road sign. it points the lost sheep to Jesus.

This miracle makes the people think of **another miracle** in the Bible. Jesus gives them food from heaven like the children of Israel in the desert. When John tells this story, he tells us what Jesus says afterwards. Jesus says: 'I am the bread of life'. 📖 *John 6:32-36.*

> ⏩ *Miracles can never satisfy us. They are like the bread. Soon we will be hungry again. But Jesus came to meet our real needs. We need him. He is the Bread of life. He satisfies us for ever.*

25 HARD HEARTS

▣ Background

In Mark 3, Jesus calls his 12 disciples. Jesus teaches them many things. He wants them to understand who he is. He sends them (in Mark 6) to tell others to repent because the Christ, their Messiah, has come.

Mark has shown us that many **leaders** of the Jews are against Jesus. The **crowds** love Jesus, but most only want his miracles. And even the **disciples** are very slow to believe in Jesus.

📖 *Mark 4:35-41 and Mark 6:45-52.* Again, the disciples are afraid. Even now, they do not understand who Jesus is. Mark 6:52 tells us why.

▢ Main point

We can know a lot about Jesus, but still have hard hearts. We need to trust Jesus for ourselves.

✶ Something to work on

It is difficult to see when our hearts are hard. Like the disciples, we think that we love Jesus. We like to come to church. But if we do not trust Jesus to be our Saviour, then our hearts become hard. [⊞ *Find a word picture to explain what a hard heart is. It means that we do not change when God's word speaks to us.*]

▣ Notes

• **Mark 6:48.** 'Fourth watch.' Between 3 and 6 in the morning.

• **Mark 6:49.** 'Ghost.' A spirit that looks like a dead person.

• **Mark 6:52.** 'Their hearts were hardened (had become hard).' Some Bibles say: 'their minds could not grasp (understand) it.'

• **Mark 6:53-56.** Jesus is very popular. Many people want him to heal them. Jesus shows them his power. But they are like the disciples. They do not understand who Jesus really is. They do not see why he has come. They just want him to heal them.

THEY WERE AFRAID

📖 *Mark 6:50*

Jesus has left the crowds (who do not understand who he is). Jesus has left the disciples (who do not understand who he is). Jesus prays alone with his Father (who understands everything). Then he goes back to the disciples, to teach them yet again who he is.

On the lake, it is hard work for the disciples... *[Tell the story.]*

• Did they need to be afraid? Why were they afraid?

They were afraid because they did not see that it was Jesus.

> ⧆ *When Jesus is with us, we do not need to be afraid! When are you afraid? When you are afraid, do you think about Jesus – or have you forgotten him?*
>
> ⧆ 📖 *Isaiah 43:1-3. Jesus promises to be with his people. We are always safe when Jesus looks after us! David said to God: 'When I am afraid, I will trust in you.' (Psalm 56:3). Can you say that?*

THEY DID NOT UNDERSTAND

📖 *Mark 6:52*

• Why did they think Jesus was a ghost? Why did they not think it was Jesus?

They did not see it was Jesus, because they did not **understand**. They knew about the time when Jesus told the waves to be still. They knew that Jesus had just fed 5,000 people with five loaves and two fish. But they did not understand who Jesus really is. So they did not think Jesus could walk on the water.

Mark tells us something shocking. 'Their hearts were hard.' They had seen so many things that showed who Jesus is. But they still had not believed. And now they just cannot see. Their hearts are too hard.

> ⧆ *We can be like the disciples. We can know so much about Jesus, but still not trust him. Then what happens? Our hearts become hard. We hear many things, but nothing changes us. Turn to Jesus **today**!*
> 📖 *Hebrews 3:12-15.*

26 JESUS SHOWS WHAT THE PHARISEES ARE REALLY LIKE

◉ Background

We have seen that the Pharisees hate Jesus. He does not keep their rules. He is too popular. He shows the people what the Pharisees are really like.

So now, some Pharisees come from Jerusalem. We will see what happens!

📖 *Mark 7:1-23.* This is a very important section. It shows us what is wrong with the Pharisees and the Jewish leaders. And it shows us what is wrong with men and women everywhere. It shows us the heart of our problem.

◉ Main point

God wants true worship. He does not want us just to **say** the right things. He wants us to love him from the heart.

◉ Something to work on

Work through the notes carefully. Your people must understand that God's laws and our rules can be different. Are there rules in your church. which do not come from the Bible? Are you very concerned about your church traditions, but you do not worry if people lie or hate or gossip?

◉ Notes

- **Mark 7:1-4.** In the market place, the Jews mixed with Gentiles. They thought that this made them 'unclean' (dirty) before God. They thought that if they then ate food, they would become 'unclean' inside. So they washed their hands in a religious way to stop this. This teaching did **not** come from the Old Testament. (It is good to wash our hands before eating. This is different, a religious custom.)

- **Mark 7:5.** 'Tradition of the elders/ancestors.' The 'elders' (leaders) made up rules or 'traditions' to help the Jews keep God's law better. It is always dangerous to add to God's laws! Our laws and traditions can become more important to us than God's laws (Mark 7:8).

- **Mark 7:6.** 'Hypocrites.' A hypocrite is someone who pretends. That means he seems different from what he really is. These people seemed to follow God, but they did not really love him. Inside, they loved themselves, not God.

- **Mark 7:11.** A Jew has some money. His parents need help. He does not want to give his money. So he says it is 'Corban'. This means that he has promised to give it to God. So he cannot help his parents.

JESUS HATES IT WHEN WE PRETEND

📖 *Mark 7:6*

These Jews thought that God was very pleased with them. They thought that they were the best! These Jews thought that they kept all God's laws, and many more as well! They thought that the disciples were the bad people, because they did not wash their hands in the proper way! *[Explain this example from Mark 7:1-4.]*

• So why does Jesus say hard things against them? Why does he say that they are 'hypocrites'?

These Jews wanted **to look good on the outside**. But God wants us to **be good on the inside**.

Think of all the things we do **that look good on the outside**. *[Go to church... sing praise... say prayers... say nice things about someone...]* When is God pleased with these things? When is he not pleased with them?

> ➠ *Jesus hates it when we pretend. He sees us on the inside. He hears what we say in our hearts. He sees what we do when no one else is looking.*
>
> • *Is Mark 7:6 true about you?*

JESUS HATES IT WHEN WE LET GO OF GOD'S COMMANDS

📖 *Mark 7:8*

⊞ Do you like it when your child pretends to obey you? He makes you think that he obeys you. But really he has his own plans. He does not really want to obey you. *[Think of an example.]*

The example Jesus chose, **showed the truth** about these Jews. They cared about **their** rules, because it made them look good. But they did not care about God's commands, because they did not love God. *[Explain the 'Corban' example Mark 7:9-13.]* They keep **their** rules (Corban) because it looks good. They do not keep God's law (honour your parents) because they do not love God.

> ➠ *Mark 7:8. Jesus' words are very strong. Does he speak to you? Do you love God's laws? Or do you only keep them when other people see you? [Give some examples.]*
>
> *Do you want other people to see that you are a good Christian, but really you do the things that make **you** happy? Do you make sure that you keep all the church traditions, but let go of God's commands? [Give some examples.]*

27 THE PROBLEM IS DEEP INSIDE US

▣ Background

📖 *Mark 7:1-13.* Jesus has shown the Pharisees that they have a big problem. They pretend to be holy, but really they want to please themselves. They say they love God, but really they love themselves. They keep many rules on the outside, but they do not obey God's commands in their hearts.

Now Jesus shows them the root of that problem. They are worried that sin will come **into** them from outside. However, **Jesus** says that we already have sin **inside**. Food from outside cannot make us 'unclean' in God's eyes. Sin coming from our hearts makes us unclean (dirty).
📖 *Mark 7:14-23.*

The heart is where the problem of sin comes from.

In the Old Testament, God promised to give his people a new heart. He promised to send a Saviour, to change us from the inside.
📖 *Ezekiel 36:26, John 3:3.*

▣ Main point

Sin comes from deep inside us. Therefore, we need God to change us inside.

⊡ Something to work on

Jesus' teaching is very important. Many people think that they must be good **only on the outside**. They try to do good things. They try to live as a Christian. However, they are like the Pharisees. They need a new heart. Pray that God will show your people that their sin is deep inside.

▣ Notes

• **Mark 7:14,17.** The Pharisees did not understand. Neither did **the crowds and the disciples**. They also needed to see that sin comes from our hearts.

• **Mark 7:19.** Food cannot make us dirty in God's eyes! The Old T food laws were like pictures for Israel, to teach them about their holy God. But Jesus shows us here that those food laws have finished. God is not worried what comes **into** our stomachs. God cares about what comes **out** of our hearts.

• **Mark 7:21.** Find out what these words mean if you can. There are bad things we **do** (like 'adultery' – sexual sin), bad things we **say** (like 'deceit' – telling lies) and bad things we **think** (like 'pride' – we think that we are better than others).

SIN DOES NOT COME FROM OUTSIDE

📖 *Mark 7:15,18-19*

⊞In some countries, people do not like dirt to come into their clean homes. They ask you to take your shoes off when you come from outside. However, inside their homes are many 'dirty' things. Bad words, bad feelings, bad programmes on television. The real dirt is inside the home. *[You may need to change this word picture to help your people.]*

The Pharisees thought that sin came from outside. They washed in this religious way so that they did not eat anything 'unclean'. But Jesus says that this is silly. Food goes into the stomach and out the other end! This has nothing to do with sin! The real dirt is inside them already.

• What other things are **outside** things, which have nothing to do with sin?

We must not let **sinful** things come into our lives from outside. Sinful things can come into our hearts and make us even worse inside.

> ⟫ 📖 *1 Samuel 16:7. Do you try to look like a Christian on the outside, but inside you still have a bad heart?*

SIN COMES FROM INSIDE

📖 *Mark 7:20-23*

Think of different sorts of sin. Where does each one start? Sin starts inside. It starts with bad thoughts. The first sin in Jesus' list is 'evil thoughts' (Mark 7:21). We are bad inside. *[Talk about the sins in Jesus' list. Show that they all come from inside. Show that every sin is really against **God**.]*

[Use examples. You want to be a Christian, so you stop stealing things. But you still want to steal things. When no one can find out, you still steal things. People think that you have changed. But inside you are still just as bad. Your heart wants to steal.]

> ⟫ *Has God spoken to you today? Do you see how bad your heart is? Then tell God about it. Say how bad you are. Say how sorry you are.*

Who can make you clean inside?

• **You cannot** change your heart. You can try to be good, but you will still be bad inside.

• **God can change** your heart. Jesus is the doctor who came for people who are bad inside (Mark 2:17). His blood is the only thing that can clean dirty hearts. That is why he came to die on the cross. Will you trust Jesus to clean your heart?
📖 1 John 1:9

28 A GENTILE WOMAN SHOWS GREAT FAITH!

▣ Background

The Jews think they are 'clean'. Jesus told them that they are not clean, because sin comes from inside.

📖 *Mark 7:1-23.*

Now Jesus turns away from the Jews and goes to a Gentile area. 'Gentiles' (or 'Greeks') are not Jews. The Jews thought that the Gentiles were not clean. However, Jesus wants to show that Gentiles are the same as Jews. Both Jews and Gentiles need God to change them **inside**.

Imagine what the disciples (who were Jews) thought when Jesus went to a Gentile town. Remember, the Jews thought that God had no interest in Gentiles.

📖 *Mark 7:24-8:10.* Some stories are like those we have already read in Mark. The big difference is that Jesus now shows the **Gentiles** who he is.

▣ Main point

Jesus accepts **anyone** who trusts in Him.

✳ Something to work on

It was hard for the disciples to see Jesus go to Gentile towns. Your people need to understand this. Does your tribe or country have old enemies? Do you look down on some people? Jesus came for these people as well as for you.

▣ Notes

- **Mark 7:24.** Jesus went to Tyre, a Gentile town. Jesus did not go to look for the Gentile people. They came to find him! Jesus' work was to show the Jews who he is. He told us to take the good news to the rest of the world.

- **Mark 7:27.** This sounds unkind, but Jesus is never rude. Jews sometimes called Gentiles 'dogs.' It meant that they had no place in God's kingdom. We know that Jesus will show his love to the woman. So his words probably mean 'You know what the Jews think of you. So why have you come to me?' Jesus does not want to put off the woman. He wants to bring out her faith in him.

GREAT NEED

📖 *Mark 7:24-28*

Jesus always accepts people who **need him**!

- See how **desperate** this woman is. She does not wait for Jesus to come out of the house. She must see him **now**!

Jesus wanted to be alone with his disciples. But he did not tell the woman to go away. He always has time for people who need him.

- See how **humble** this woman is. She does not mind when Jesus says Mark 7:27. She does not say: 'I am as good as any Jew!' She knows that she does not deserve anything from Jesus. Are you like her?

> ➲ *It does not matter who you are. It does not matter how bad you are. It does not matter if you do not come from a Christian family.*
>
> **If you know that you need Jesus, Jesus will not send you away.**

GREAT FAITH

Jesus always accepts people who **put their trust in him**!

- See how she '**begs**' Jesus. ('Beg' means 'ask very strongly'.) She does not say: 'Perhaps you can help me.' She **knows** that Jesus can drive out the demon. She begs Jesus, because only Jesus can do this.

- See how she **keeps on asking**. When Jesus tests her faith, she does not give up. She does not mind being a 'dog', if she can have the crumbs from the table!

- See how she **accepts what Jesus says** (Mark 7:29). She is happy to go home, because she trusts Jesus. She expects to find her daughter well.

Remember that the disciples are watching Jesus. They have not often seen **Jews** believe like this! But this **Gentile** woman believes!

> ➲ *It does not matter who you are. It does not matter if other people do not want you. Jesus accepts **anyone** who trusts in him. Will you be like this woman? Will you bring your great need to Jesus? Will you beg him to save you? Will you believe his promise?*
>
> 📖 *John 6:35*
>
> ➲ *Jesus is willing to accept **anyone** who wants to trust him. How about you? Do you look down on some people or think they are no good? We must welcome anyone and everyone.*

29 A MIRACLE WITH A MESSAGE

◉ Background

Jesus is now in a Gentile area. The Jews have not understood who Jesus is. Will the Gentiles understand?

Even the **disciples** do not really understand. It is like they are deaf. Jesus teaches them, but they still do not believe that he is the Son of God (Mark 7:18).

📖 *Mark 8:1-10.* This is like the last time they had no food. But the disciples have forgotten what happened! 📖 *Mark 8:17-18, 21.*

The miracle in Mark 7:31-37 is not just another miracle. It is a miracle with a **message**. It teaches the disciples, who are deaf in another way.

◉ Main point

We need a miracle too! We need Jesus to open our ears so that we can believe. We need Jesus to open our mouths so that we can tell people about him.

⊡ Something to work on

This miracle is like a picture to teach the disciples. The miracle is not really harder than all his other ones. So why does Jesus make this miracle seem like a big thing? Why does Jesus sigh? Why is he sad?

Jesus sees that the people and his disciples are like this deaf man. It is like they are deaf to God's truth. They too need a miracle. They need a miracle to change their hearts. Think how you can explain this to your people.

◉ NOTES

- **Mark 7:31.** 'Decapolis' or 'Ten towns' was a Gentile area. 📖 *Mark 5:20.*

- **Mark 7:34.** 'Deep sigh'/'groan.' Jesus is very sad and upset. Why? It is not just because the man is deaf. The big problem is that the people do not believe in him (Mark 8:12).

- **Mark 7:36.** Jesus did not want people to speak about his miracles. He did not want them to give the wrong message about him. Jesus is not just 'the man who does miracles'! If they really knew who Jesus was, they would **obey** him.

JESUS IS SAD

📖 *Mark 7:34*

Jesus is sad about the deaf man. Jesus is always sad when we are in trouble. Jesus is sad about the disease and pain in the world. However, he is more sad when people do not believe in him. *[Explain how this man is like a picture of the disciples, and us, when we do not 'hear' who Jesus really is.]*

> » *When Jesus looks at you, does he sigh? Is he sad because you know so much about him, but it does not go into your heart?*

> » *Would you like to be deaf? Of course not! But it is much worse to be 'deaf' to Jesus' words (spiritually deaf). Do you care about that?*

JESUS DOES A MIRACLE

📖 *Mark 7:33-35*

First Jesus shows that he can heal this man. The man cannot hear, so Jesus does things that he can see. He puts his fingers in the man's ear and touches his tongue. Now the man knows that Jesus will heal him.

Next Jesus shows the man that he needs God's miracle. So Jesus looks up to heaven. Then he tells the man's ears and tongue to open. And they do!

> » *A deaf person cannot make himself hear! We cannot make ourselves believe. We need God's miracle. It is not enough to hear about Jesus. We need Jesus to open our ears so that we can understand. We need Jesus to open our mouths so that we can tell people who Jesus really is.*

> *Will you ask Jesus to do that? Ask for yourself. Ask for your friends.*

JESUS IS WONDERFUL!

📖 *Read Mark 7:34*

These people told everyone about Jesus. They thought he was wonderful.

- Should they have told people about Jesus? Or should they have kept quiet?

They did not really love Jesus. They did not obey him. If we love Jesus, we will obey him.

> » *If you think that Jesus is wonderful, then first you must* **obey** *him. Do not tell people how good Jesus is, if you will not do what Jesus says.*

> » *When Jesus saves us and changes us, he does not tell us to keep quiet. Now he wants us to tell others the truth about our wonderful Jesus.*

30 BREAD FROM HEAVEN – AGAIN!

▣ Background

Mark can only tell us **a few** stories about Jesus. So why does he include **two** stories about bread from heaven? 📖 *Mark 6:30-44 and Mark 8:1-10*. See how many things are the same.

Remember that Mark does not just want to tell us **what happened**. He has a **message** for us. It is Mark's 'gospel' (good news). So why does he tell us about bread from heaven **again**?

Remember that now Jesus is in a **Gentile** (non-Jewish) area. He wants to teach the disciples who he really is. He wants to show them that he is Saviour. He is Saviour of the **world**, not just of **the Jews**. 📖 *Mark 8:11-21*. This shows that Jesus wants them to **understand** the miracle. He wants them to see who he is.

So Jesus does the same miracle for the Gentiles. This is **to show the disciples who he is**.

▣ Main point

Jesus is the Saviour who has come for everyone, not just Jews.

⊠ Something to work on

The story is almost the same as in Mark 6. This is what Mark wants us to see! Do not just tell the miracle in the same way as last time. Show why Jesus feeds the Gentiles, as well as the Jews.

▣ Notes

• If you have a Bible map, try to follow Jesus' journey through the Gentile area. He went to **Tyre** (Mark 7:24), then to **Decapolis** (Mark 7:31). Then Jesus went back to **Dalmanutha** (Mark 8:10) on the Jewish side of the lake.

• **Mark 8:8.** The word Mark uses for 'basket' is different from Mark 6:43. This is because the Gentiles used a different kind of basket from the Jews.

THE SAME LOVE

📖 *Mark 8:1-3*

Do you care a lot about some people, and not so much about other people? Maybe you would not mind if some people were hungry. Perhaps you do not like them. Or perhaps you think they have little value.

Jesus shows the **same love** for these Gentile people as for his own people. He cares just as much that they are hungry. He feeds 4,000 Gentiles in the same way as he fed 5,000 Jewish people in Mark 6. *[Talk more about this. Show Jesus' care for these people. Show how it is like the miracle in Mark 6.]*

• Imagine what the disciples thought of this. Remember that they did not respect the Gentiles. They thought that God only cared about the Jews. Imagine what they thought when they had to serve these Gentile people (Mark 8:6).

> ⏩ *Jesus wants the disciples to understand who he is. Do you understand who Jesus is? He is the Saviour who cares about **every kind** of person. He cares for the people that you do not like. He cares for the children and the old people. He cares for the women as much as he cares for the men.*

> ⏩ *Do you want Jesus to be your Saviour? Do you want Jesus to be the Saviour of those you do not like?*

THE SAME REACTION

📖 *Mark 8:4-10*

The disciples were the same as before.

📖 *Mark 8:4.* No one said: 'Why not give them food from heaven, like last time?' They think that it is impossible to feed this crowd! This is because they still do not see who Jesus is. 📖 *Mark 8:21.*

The people were the same as before.

📖 *Mark 8:8,9.* They were all full. They were happy that Jesus had fed them. However, they were happy to go away from Jesus. They were just like the 5,000 Jews who Jesus fed. They liked the miracle. But they did not see who Jesus was. They did not think: *'If Jesus makes bread and fish for us, he must be God. He must have come for us!'* Therefore, they did not follow Jesus. They just went home.

> ⏩ *We hear many things about Jesus. We like to hear them.*
>
> *We believe the stories. However, do we really see who Jesus is? If we do, then how will it show?*

31 BLIND AND DEAF, WITH HARD HEARTS

◉ Background

Soon the disciples will see who Jesus is; 📖 *Mark 8:29*. At last they will understand! So **how** will they understand?

Mark shows us that the disciples need a **miracle**. In Mark 8:11-21, they still cannot see who Jesus is. Their hearts are still hard. They do not believe. Notice how they are like the Pharisees! 📖 *Mark 3:5; 6:52; 7:17, 18*.

Now read 📖 *Mark 8:11, 12, 15, 17, 18, 21*.

◉ Main point

Like the disciples, our hearts are hard. We too need a miracle so that we believe in Jesus.

✴ Something to work on

It is difficult to think that **we** can be like people who hate Jesus. But Jesus warns his disciples not to be like the Pharisees and Herod. The disciples do not hate Jesus, but they do have the same **hard hearts** as Jesus' enemies.

What about **our hearts**? Are we the same as people who have no time for Jesus? Help your people to see that they need a miracle to change their hearts.

◉ Notes

• **Mark 8:15.** People use 'yeast' to bake bread. It makes the bread rise. A little yeast spreads through all the bread mixture. This is a picture. Jesus tells the disciples 'Be careful! The **'yeast'** of the Pharisees will spread to you. You will get the same **hard hearts**.'.

• **Mark 8:15:.**'Herod.' Herod was the Roman Ruler of the region. The Romans did not believe in the God of the Jews. So they did not believe in Jesus.

WATCH OUT!

📖 *Mark 8:11-15*

We can become like the people close to us!

- Who have you become like? Perhaps your husband or wife? Your parents or your friend? We can start to think like them and talk like them.

Jesus says: 'Be careful! Watch out!' The disciples knew that the Pharisees hated Jesus, but there was still danger. The disciples have started to think like the Pharisees.

- Who are the people who think wrong things about Jesus? (People on the television or radio, politicians, teachers, friends?) Have you started to think like them about Jesus?

How did the Pharisees think?
📖 *Mark 8:11, 12.* Jesus was sad, because he saw how hard their hearts were. They did not want to believe in him. They just wanted to test Jesus. They wanted to turn people against Jesus.

> ➨ *Jesus says: 'Be careful of that yeast!' It can easily spread to us. We can be like the people around us.* **We can have hard hearts. We can be very slow to believe in Jesus.**

HARD HEARTS

📖 *Mark 8:16-21*

The disciples did not understand Jesus. They thought that he was talking about bread! Jesus asks two questions;

1. 'Do you not remember?'
📖 *Mark 8:18-20*

Of course the disciples remembered what happened! **But they had not learnt the lesson.** They still did not believe who Jesus was!

> ➨ *Do you remember the things that you have learnt about Jesus? And does that change you? Do you* **trust in** *Jesus now?*

2. 'Do you still not understand?'
📖 *Mark 8:18-20*

No, they did not understand. They were like blind men, or deaf men. They had seen Jesus do so much, they had heard Jesus say so much. But they still did not understand. Their hearts were still hard. They needed a miracle.

> ➨ *Perhaps you know much about Jesus. But has Jesus done a miracle in your heart?*
>
> *Has Jesus changed you inside and given you faith to believe in him?*
>
> *If not, ask him now!*

32 PETER SEES!

⊡ Background

The disciples are still blind. They cannot see who Jesus is. They need a miracle.

The next thing we read is a miracle! 📖 **Mark 8:22-26.** A blind man sees. It is another miracle with a **message** (like Mark 7:31-35). Straight after this miracle, Peter shows that he now sees! He sees that Jesus is the Christ, the Saviour. 📖 **Mark 8:27-30.**

Mark 8:29 answers the big question of Mark 1-8. 'Who is Jesus?' **Jesus is the Christ!**

The rest of Mark answers another big question. 'Why did Jesus come?'

WHO JESUS IS	WHY JESUS CAME
Mark chapters 1-8	Mark chapters 9-16

⊡ Main point

Peter says that Jesus is the Christ.

⊡ Notes

• **Mark 8:23,26.** Jesus takes the man out of the village. Jesus does not want him to go back to the village afterwards. This is because Jesus wants to keep this miracle quiet. It is a miracle for the **disciples** to think about.

• **Mark 8:23-25.** Why does Jesus touch the man's eyes **twice**? It is not because Jesus' miracle did not work well the first time. Jesus **meant** to do the miracle in two parts, because the miracle has a **message**.

This man is **like the disciples.** Very soon, they will see – but they will only half see! Peter sees that Jesus is the Christ, but he does not see that Jesus must die. (Mark 8:31, 32). Peter is like the man in Mark 8:24. For the rest of Mark, the disciples are still half-blind. Jesus teaches them, but they do not see very well. They do not completely understand until Jesus rises from the dead.

• **Mark 8:29.** Peter sees that Jesus is the **Christ** (Messiah), who God promised in the Old Testament. He sees that God has sent Jesus to save his people.

• **Mark 8:30.** They must not tell people yet, because people have the wrong idea about 'the Christ'. They first need to see what the Christ came to do.

AN IMPORTANT QUESTION

📖 *Mark 8:23,27,29*

⊕ We all like to see! How do you feel if you cannot see something? Imagine how much a blind person wants to see.

Jesus has done a miracle. This blind man starts to see. Then Jesus asks him an important question. 'Do you see anything?' He was so excited – he began to see people!

Jesus asks **the disciples** an important question. So far, they have been blind. Now do they see? Are they like all the other blind people, who do not see who Jesus is?
📖 *Mark 8:27, 28.*

Or are they different now – do they see at last? 📖 *Mark 8:29.*

> ⨠ *Jesus asks us the same question today. Other people have many ideas about Jesus, but Jesus asks you. What do you say about Jesus? Has Jesus opened your eyes yet? Do you see things now that you did not understand before? When someone asks you, what will you say?*

AN IMPORTANT ANSWER

📖 *Mark 8:29*

'I can see!' Those are the best words a blind man ever said! From now on, his whole life changes.

'You are the Christ!' Those are the best words Peter ever said! Now he knew that it was true. And he knew that it was important. God had sent the Saviour, and Peter believed in him. Other people say different things about Jesus, but Peter knows the truth. And Peter is not afraid to say it.

> ⨠ *Do you believe that Jesus is the Christ, God's Saviour? And is it important to you? Is it so important that it changes your life? Is it so important that you are happy to tell others? And, because Jesus is the Saviour, you will trust him and follow him, like Peter.*

> ⨠ *Perhaps you are like Peter. You only half-see. There are still many things that you do not understand. Start with the things that you **do** understand. Do not be afraid to tell others that you believe in Jesus the Saviour. And, as you follow Jesus, he will help you to see more and more.*

33 THE WAY OF THE CROSS

◉ Background

The disciples now see who Jesus is. Peter has said: 'You are the Christ.'

But they only half see. They do not understand what 'the Christ' came to do. They imagine that Jesus will now lead the Jews against the Romans. They think that Jesus will set himself up as their King in Jerusalem. They hope that they will have important jobs in Jerusalem.

But they are wrong. They need to listen to Jesus. And they need to follow 'the Christ' in the path that he leads them on.

The second half of Mark will show us **what Christ came to do.**

◉ Main point

A true *Christ*ian follows *Christ* in the way of the cross.

✦ Something to work on

Many people like to say that they are Christians. Jesus shows us that we are only Christians if we follow Jesus in the way of the cross. People do not want to believe this. Many people want to have an easy Christian life. They hope that Jesus will give them many nice things. They want to follow Jesus in their **own** way. Jesus says that they are wrong. There is only one way to be a Christian, and that is **Jesus'** way.

• How can you make this clear to your people?

This section is very important. You can do more than one talk on it.

◉ Notes

• **Mark 8:31.** Jesus calls himself the 'Son of Man'. He does not just mean that he is a man! Jesus means that he is the powerful 'Son of Man' who Daniel spoke about. 📖 *Daniel 7:13, 14.* Jesus will go to the cross, but remember this. Jesus **is** God's powerful King. And he will rule over everything!

• **Mark 8:33.** Jesus calls Peter 'Satan' because he speaks against God's plan. Peter is thinking like Satan, not like God. Peter needs to accept God's plan for Jesus. Jesus must go to the cross and Peter must not try to stop him. Jesus 'rebukes' Peter (tells Peter that he was wrong).

WHAT KIND OF CHRIST?

📖 *Mark 8:31-33*

⊕ Who do you want to be like? Who is your hero? Who do you think is great?

We want to follow someone who is strong, someone who will win. No one follows a man who people hate and kill! We are like the disciples. The disciples wanted to help King Jesus rule the world. They did not want to go to the cross with him.

Can you understand Peter? He sees that Jesus is God's King, the 'Christ'. So how can Jesus **fail**? How can Jesus die? Peter thinks that is impossible!

Jesus is a different kind of king, a different kind of hero. Because Jesus let people kill him on a cross, he is great. Because Jesus died for our sins, we follow him. One day we will all see that Jesus is King. Jesus will come back as a powerful King (Mark 8:38). But first, people reject him (push him away). They will not have Jesus as their king. They kill him on the cross.

> ⨠ *Will you follow this Jesus? Will you follow Jesus, who people hate? When people say bad things about Jesus, will you say 'Jesus is my Saviour and king?'*

WHAT KIND OF CHRISTIAN?

📖 *Mark 8:34-38*

There is only one kind of true Christian. A *Christ*ian follows *Christ*. Christ went to the cross. Jesus tells us what that means for us. *[Think of word pictures for each point. Think what these things meant for the disciples. Think what these things mean for us, in real life.]*

- **Jesus not self;** 📖 *Mark 8:34.* When I say yes to Jesus, I say no to myself. I do not become a Christian because it will be better for **me**! I follow **Jesus**, whatever it costs me.
- **The cross, not life;** 📖 *Mark 8:34, 35.* I give up my life to Jesus. I do not hold on to **my** time, **my** needs, **my** family, **my** life. Because I belong to Jesus, I am willing to suffer. Because Jesus went to the cross, I am willing to die for him.
- **The gospel, not the world;** 📖 *Mark 8:35, 36.* When I follow Jesus, I do not want to have a big house or lots of money. These things are not important because Jesus has saved my 'soul' (the real me that lives for ever). What matters now is to tell people the gospel. Everyone needs to know about Jesus.

> ⨠ *Are you this kind of Christian? There is no other kind. If we do not follow Jesus in this way of the cross, what will he feel about us?*
> 📖 *Mark 8:38*

34 A SPECIAL SHOW

▣ Background

The disciples at last see that Jesus is the Christ, the Son of God. Now, in the second half of Mark, Jesus shows them that the Christ must **die**. He also shows them that they must be willing to give up their lives. He has told them this in **Mark 8:31-38.** Now Jesus will teach them more.

Here is the first lesson for three disciples. Jesus will **show them his power and glory**. Jesus' plan to go to the cross is not a big mistake. Jesus **is** God's Son. He has power! He will be King in God's kingdom, **after** the cross. 📖 *Mark 9:1-13.*

⊙ Main point

Jesus is God's Son. He has power to overcome death and rise again. So listen to him! Trust what he says!

✦ Something to work on

Remember – the disciples are afraid. They do not understand what Jesus has said about the cross. Jesus wants them to believe what he says, but it does not make sense to them. Help your listeners to see that we must always believe the Bible. Think about when this is hard for them.

⊙ Notes

• **Mark 9:1.** Something will happen to show the disciples Jesus' power. Jesus may mean that they will see his power when he rises from the dead, or when he sends the Holy Spirit, or when he judges Jerusalem in AD70. We do not know. The point is that they will **see Jesus' power.** Now Jesus will help three of them to believe that. That is why he takes them up the mountain.

• **Mark 9:2-3.** Christians sometimes call this event *'The Transfiguration'*. This means that Jesus changed what he looked like. He shone so brightly that it hurt to look at him.

• **Mark 9:4. Elijah** and *Moses* represent the **prophets** and the *Law*. It is as if the Old Testament stands there with Jesus. Elijah and Moses agree with Jesus.

• **Mark 9:11-13.** In the Old Testament, Malachi says that Elijah will come before the Christ. Jesus says that Elijah **has** come. Jesus taught that John the Baptist was the 'Elijah' who Malachi spoke about (Matthew 11:14).

JESUS REALLY IS GOD'S SON!
📖 *Mark 9:2-7*

⊕ Have you ever been to a special show or festival? *[Think of an example.]* You saw some wonderful things. You enjoyed it so much.

Jesus took three of his disciples to a special Show. It was more wonderful than any show we have been to! But Jesus did not do this for fun. It was to help the disciples understand two things.

1. Jesus will die on the cross.
2. Jesus is God's Son.
Jesus wanted the disciples to believe both things together.

• How did what happened on the mountain teach them this?

At first they did not understand much. They were so frightened that they said the wrong thing.
📖 *Mark 9:5, 6.* But they did hear what God said from heaven.
📖 *Mark 9:7.* And they would never forget Jesus' glory and power. He shone so white, so bright. What Peter had said (Mark 8:29) must be right – Jesus is the Christ, the King, the Son of God.

⏩ *Jesus wants us to believe these two things. 1. He did die a terrible death on the cross. 2. And he really is the Son of God.*

He is the King, and one day we will see him shining bright. Do you believe these things about Jesus?

SO LISTEN TO HIM!
📖 *Mark 9:7-10*

• *Who do you listen to? Who do you believe? Who do you trust?*

The disciples were slow to believe Jesus. Peter even argued with him and told him off! (Mark 8:32) Now God tells them from heaven: 'Listen to my Son!' Elijah and Moses are there too. It is as if God says to the disciples: 'The Old Testament agrees with Jesus.' The disciples believe the Old Testament. But they are not ready to believe everything that Jesus says.

They must believe Jesus when he says that he will die. They must believe Jesus when he says that he will rise from the dead. That is hard. It is so different from what they think.

⏩ *We too must **always** believe what Jesus says in the Bible.*

⏩ *Remember God's voice from heaven! Listen to God's Son! One day Jesus will come back. He will shine like the sun. And he will want to know if you listened to him. [Challenge your listeners with this.]*

35 NO FAITH, NO POWER

▣ Background

The main thing Jesus wants to teach his disciples is this – their Messiah must **die**. 📖 *Mark 8:31.* Jesus says it again in Mark 9:31 (and Mark 10:33, 34).

How does **Mark 9:14-29** fit? How does it teach the disciples to believe Jesus?

Jesus has just shown three disciples **his power.**

They must listen to Jesus and trust his plan. 📖 *Mark 9:1-13.*

Now Jesus comes down the mountain to find the other disciples. How have they done without him? 📖 *Mark 9:14-29.* They have not put their faith in him!

▣ Main point

We can do nothing without faith in Jesus.

⊞ Something to work on

1. Only Jesus has the power to heal. Only Jesus has the power to tell evil spirits to go. We can **ask** Jesus to heal or tell an evil spirit to go. We cannot do this ourselves. 📖 *Mark 9:29.*

Do you need to explain this to your listeners?

2. Sometimes people tell us that we need big faith. This father shows us that the important thing is **Jesus'** power. Always help your listeners to look to Jesus, not at themselves.

▣ Notes

• **Mark 9:17, 18, 20.** This man has an evil spirit. This is not the same as the illness we call epilepsy. Epilepsy can look similar to Mark 9:18. We must not think that a person has an evil spirit when he has epilepsy. Epilepsy needs medicine.

NO FAITH IN JESUS, NO POWER!

📖 *Mark 9:14-19*

Jesus has just been up the mountain. Three of his disciples have seen his great power. Now they come down the mountain. What do they find?

It looks as if the devil is in control. The boy has a terrible evil spirit, the other disciples can do nothing, and the crowds argue!

The disciples have no power against the evil spirit, **because they have no faith in Jesus.** 📖 *Mark 9:18, 19*.

The problem is that they do not believe Jesus. He told them that he will die and rise from the dead. But they do not believe him. If we do not believe in Jesus' death and resurrection, we can have no power. Jesus' death and resurrection is the only power that defeats the devil!

> ⟩⟩ *The devil wants to be in control of your life. He does not often come inside people like this poor boy, but he does control us in other ways. [Explain these ways. Examples: fear of sorcery, love of money.] If you do not have faith in Jesus, you can have no power against the devil.*

> ⟩⟩ *Many of us do believe in Jesus. But sadly, we forget to put faith in him. Then we have no power in our lives. We are like a radio without a battery, or a television without electricity. We need to pray, and to trust Jesus' power.* 📖 ***Mark 9:29.***

FAITH IN JESUS, HEALED BOY!

📖 *Mark 9:20-29*

This poor father does not know if Jesus has enough power! Of course Jesus does! But does the father have enough **faith** in his power? 📖 *Mark 9:22, 23.*

• How much faith does the man have to show? 📖 *Mark 9:24.*

The father may not believe completely, but Jesus is glad to see his faith. Straight away, Jesus tells the evil spirit to go, and the boy is well.

> ⟩⟩ *Do you feel that your faith is weak? Do you feel like this man? Do not be afraid. Say sorry to Jesus that your faith is weak. And begin to put your weak faith in your strong Jesus. Do not think a lot about how weak **you** are. Think a lot about **Jesus**. Trust his great love and his great power. He will hear you! Then his power will work in your life.*

36 BIG OR LITTLE?

◉ Background

The disciples have seen that Jesus is the Christ. Now Jesus wants his disciples to know what kind of Christ he is. So...

- Jesus tells them again about his plan to die. 📖 *Mark 9:30-32.*

- Jesus teaches them again about what they must be like. If they will follow Christ, they must be like him. They must be willing to be little. 📖 *Mark 9:33-41.*

This is the background for Mark 8, 9 and 10. Both these points are hard for the disciples to understand. They are so different from what the disciples expect. Jesus has to teach these things many times.
📖 *Mark 8-10.*

◉ Main point

Jesus calls Christians to be servants, to be little, to be last.

✦ Something to work on

This is hard to preach about. In most churches, there are people who think that they are important. Often they are people who have money or land. Or they are elders or deacons.

It is hard for these people to accept Jesus' words. Pray that God will help you to preach the truth. Ask him to help you to be gentle. Pray that God will help 'big' people to become 'little' people.

Perhaps you too need to learn this lesson. If we preach God's word, we are God's servants. We are not important. We want people to love Jesus. We must not put ourselves up above our people.

◉ Notes

- **Mark 9:36, 37.** Jesus does not love children more than adults. He uses the children to teach a lesson. Jesus wants us to welcome anyone who is happy to be little. A 'little child' means a person who is like a little child. He does not mind what people think of him. Jesus welcomes people like this to belong to him. We are like Jesus if we welcome 'little' people to Jesus. Jesus says it is like welcoming him!
📖 *Mark 10:13-16.*

IS JESUS BIG OR LITTLE?

📖 *Mark 9:30-32*

We know that Jesus is the greatest person ever! However, Jesus became **little**. Jesus let everyone think that he was nothing. Even one of his own disciples gave him away to the enemy ('betrayed' him). Jesus let people hate him and kill him on a cross. **He became that kind of Christ.**

>> *Do you love Jesus for that? Praise Jesus that he became nothing.*

ARE WE BIG OR LITTLE?

📖 *Mark 9:33-35*

• When you read about the disciples, how do you feel?

Jesus had just told them how 'little' he was going to become. Now the disciples wanted to become 'big'. How sad Jesus felt!

The disciples wanted to be important people in Jesus' kingdom. They wanted the best jobs. They wanted everyone to know that they were special. We can be just the same. *[Talk about the ways in which we can be like this.]*

>> *Do you want to please **Jesus** most? Then he says we must become 'last' and 'servants'. Like him. [Talk about how that will show.]*

DO WE WELCOME BIG PEOPLE OR LITTLE PEOPLE?

📖 *Mark 9:36-41*

Like the disciples, we can make plans to become important. But Jesus does not want this. He does not want us to think about ourselves. He wants us to care for the people who matter to him. Who is that?

If we are 'little', like Jesus, we will welcome 'little' people. *[Explain that Jesus does not just mean children.]* The disciples thought that Jesus was far too important to notice children! But Jesus wants us to notice **everyone**. He wants us to welcome the 'little' people.

>> *Think of people who no one cares about. Jesus cares about them! He wants us to tell them the good news. We must welcome them to Jesus.*

Do you understand John in Mark 9:38? John knows that he has not welcomed this man – and John thinks that he is right! John wants to keep the power for himself. But Jesus wants us to welcome anyone who serves him.

37 THE DANGER OF HELL

◉ Background

The disciples want to be 'big' people. Jesus wants them to be 'little'. The disciples must not think that they are at the top of Jesus' kingdom. Jesus wants them to see that everyone is important to him. Jesus even cares about little children. 📖 *Mark 9:33-41.*

The way that the disciples think is very **dangerous**—
📖 *Mark 9:42-50.*

◉ Main point

Make sure that you do not go to hell. It is better to lose everything than to go to hell.

⊡ Something to work on

We do not want to make a true Christian afraid. A true Christian will not go to hell. But we need to warn other people. Some people think that they have been Christians for many years. However, they will go to hell unless they change the way they think.

◉ Notes

• **Mark 9:42.** People used a millstone to make flour from grain. It was a heavy stone.

• **Mark 9:43-47.** This is a picture of how strong we must be against sin. Jesus wants us to do everything possible to stop sin. Sin is very dangerous. It leads to hell. Jesus **does not** want us to hurt ourselves. If we cut off our hand, it will not stop us doing wrong. Jesus teaches that sin comes from **inside**, from our hearts.
📖 *Mark 7:21.*

• **Mark 9:49.** 'Everyone will be purified (made clean) by fire as a sacrifice is purified by salt' (GNB). God is like a fire. He is pure and holy. We can only be ready to face God if Jesus has made us clean.

• **Mark 9:50.** A lump of salt can lose all its salt flavour! The rain washes out the salt and leaves rubbish. We can be like that. We can look like 'salt' but have no salt in us. We can look like a Christian, but not be like Jesus at all.

DO NOT HURT MY LITTLE ONES!

📖 *Mark 9:42*

⊕ *Think how animals get very angry if you attack their babies.*

Jesus is like that with his 'little ones'. Every person who believes in him is precious and special. Jesus is very angry if we hurt them.

Have you ever tripped or pushed someone, and made them fall over? What things can do that to a young Christian? What things make them fall into sin? Or what things turn them away from Jesus? (Answers – we can be a bad example, we can be unkind, gossip...)

Why did Jesus warn the disciples? The disciples think that they are too important. They **will not welcome** Jesus' little ones. This will keep the little ones away from Jesus. If the disciples do not change, Jesus will be very angry! It would be better to drown in the sea than to make Jesus angry.

DO NOT GO TO HELL!

📖 *Mark 9:43-50*

The disciples still have the wrong idea. If they do not change, they will go to hell. They are in great danger. The disciples still want to be the most important people in Jesus' kingdom. They need to cut this out. If you want to be important, then you cannot **enter** Jesus' kingdom. This means that you go to hell.

> ⏩ *What do you think? Is it better to become **nothing** than to go to hell? Is it better to lose a leg or an eye than to go to hell? Is it better for people to hate you than to go to hell?*

[Talk about what hell is like.
📖 *Mark 9:48. Be gentle but serious. Do not shout. Show your listeners that you love them and do not want them to go to hell. Hell is a fire that never stops burning. Hell is pain that never stops hurting. It is like a worm that eats you inside.]*

📖 *Mark 9:50.* We need to be **real** Christians. It is no good to look like salt if you have no salt flavour. Everyone may think that you are a Christian, but you need to be a Christian on the **inside**. Or else you will go to hell.

> ⏩ *Think and pray. What stops you from being a real Christian? What needs to be 'cut out'? It will be painful, but **do not go to hell!***

38 DO NOT DIVORCE!

▣ Background

Jesus wants to teach **the disciples**. He wants them to understand who the Christ is. And he wants them to understand how to follow the Christ.

We have seen that they must learn to be **little**. 📖 *Mark 9:33-50.* Jesus will teach them this lesson again. 📖 *Mark 10:13-16.*

We have learned that sin is very serious. 📖 *Mark 9:42-48.* No one who follows Jesus can be careless about sin.

So what about sin in **marriage**? 📖 *Mark 10:1-12.*

⊡ Main point

Jesus wants Christians to obey God's laws. God does not want us to divorce.

✱ Something to work on

We are like the disciples. We can listen too much to what other people say and do. Other people get divorced, so we (wrongly) think that we can end our marriage too. Jesus teaches us that God's word has not changed. We must not make excuses. We must keep our marriage promises.

Think how you can help the people to value what **God** says about this.

▣ Notes

• **Mark 10:2.** This was a question to trap Jesus. The Pharisees did not really want to know the truth.

• **Mark 10:3, 4.** 📖 *Deuteronomy 24:1-4.* They must not change what Moses meant! Moses did not accept divorce! But divorce happened. God, through Moses, allowed divorce **to stop worse things**. God's clear words about marriage are in Genesis 2:24. 📖 *Mark 10:7, 8.*

• **Mark 10:11, 12.** God does not accept divorce. If we end our marriage and marry someone else, we break the seventh commandment. This is because we sleep with another person. (Matthew 19:9. If our husband or wife has slept with someone else, then we can marry again.)

WE MUST HATE SIN
📖 *Mark 10:1-5*

• Some Christians think like this: *'Jesus will forgive me, so it does not matter if I do this sin'.* How would you answer them?

Jesus hates sin just as much as his Father does! Jesus **is** God. People who follow Jesus must hate sin. We must not be like these Pharisees. We must not try to avoid God's commands. We must not make excuses.

• What does Jesus say is wrong with the Jews? 📖 *Mark 10:5*

> ➢ *We do not want to have hard hearts! Ask God to help you to love his commands. All God's commands are good – they help us to live in the best way.*

DO NOT DIVORCE
📖 *Mark 10:6-12*

Jesus says, 'Do not divorce' because God has always said 'Do not divorce.' Jesus never changed any of God's laws, because they are perfect.

• What is God's plan for man and woman? 📖 *Mark 10:6-8.*

• What command do we break if we divorce and marry again? 📖 *Mark 10:11, 12.*

• So what does Jesus tell us? 📖 *Mark 10:9.*

Jesus' words are not hard to understand. Do you find them hard to **accept**? The disciples found it hard. They asked Jesus about it again. 📖 *Mark 10:10.* Jesus says that we must keep God's word. If we want to be a Christian, we must follow what Jesus says.

[your listeners may have questions. It is important to answer them. Here are some examples:]

• **What if I have lost my love for my husband/wife?** This is no reason to divorce. Try hard to love. Show love in practical ways. Pray for God's help.

• **What if my husband/wife has slept with someone else?** Jesus says that you may divorce (and marry again). But, if you can, try to make your marriage good again.

• **I have sinned. I have divorced my husband/wife. Will God forgive me?** Yes! He forgives all sin. Try to please Him now. Do not marry again. If you have married again, try hard to make this marriage good.

• **I have two wives. What shall I do?** This is a difficult question. It is wrong to have two wives. But you must provide for both wives. You have made promises to them.

39 ACCEPT GOD'S GIFT LIKE CHILDREN

◉ Background

What kind of person enters God's kingdom? What kind of person follows Jesus? So far, the disciples have not understood.

📖 *Mark 9:33-37.* Look at Mark 9:37. Now think about Mark 10:13.

What was wrong with the way the disciples thought? We see their wrong thinking many times in Mark. 📖 *Mark 9:35.*

◉ Main point

If you want to get to heaven, you must be like a child. You must accept God's gift.

✷ Something to work on

God thinks that children are as important as adults. How can we help people understand this?

People like to think that they are important. However, Jesus wants us to become like the least important people. Pray that God will help your listeners to become like children.

◉ Notes

- **Mark 10:13.** The disciples 'rebuked' or 'scolded' the people. That means that they were not happy with the people, so they told them off. However, Jesus tells off his disciples!

- **Mark 10:14.** When Jesus talks about 'little children', he is using a picture. We must be **like** little children. (📖 *See Mark 9:42*) Children, like all people, are important to Jesus.

JESUS SAYS THAT CHILDREN ARE IMPORTANT!

 *Mark 10:14*

Think of some different people in your village. People with different jobs, adults and children, men and women. Who do you think is most important? Who do you think is not very important?

- Do people want to be the important ones?

- What do important people think of less important ones?

- 📖 *Mark 10:13.* How do the important people think about children? 📖 *Mark 10:14.* What does Jesus say?

- So who does Jesus think is important?

> ⏵ *Jesus knows that everyone is equal. He does not like us to think that we are better than children – or anyone else. Do people in your village or church think that they are better than other people are? Why do they think this way?*

JESUS SAYS THAT WE MUST BE LIKE CHILDREN!

📖 *Mark 10:15*

Proud people cannot get to heaven. People who think they are important cannot get to heaven. We must be like **children** to get to heaven.

How do we get to heaven? Look at the word Jesus uses in Mark 10:15. **'Accept,' or 'recieve'.** We must **accept** a gift like a child accepts a gift. That is how to get to heaven.

Think how children accept gifts. They are not proud. They do not think that they are too bad to get a gift. They take it quickly! They do not try to pay for their gift. They **just take it.** They have a happy smile. They say thank you!

> ⏵ *The only way to heaven is to accept everything God gives us. We must be like children.*
>
> **What does this mean?**
> - *The least important child in the village can accept God's gift.*
> - *The worst person can accept God's gift.*
> - *Our knowledge, or good works, or baptism can never buy God's gift to us.*
> *We are all the same. We all need to accept a free gift from God.*

40 A RICH MAN WHO THINKS HE IS VERY GOOD

◾ Background

Jesus has **just told us** how to enter heaven. 📖 *Mark 10:14-15*. Is the rich man like a little child? 📖 *Mark 10:17-22*.

Later, Jesus teaches about rich people. Can they enter heaven? 📖 *Mark 10:23-31*. Mark 10:31 is how Jesus finishes this teaching.

◉ Main point

Some people think that they are nearly good enough for God. Jesus shows them that they are wrong.

✦ Something to work on

What does God think of our good points? How can we help people understand that we cannot reach God's standards?

◉ Notes

- **Mark 10:18.** Jesus wants the man to understand how hard it is to be 'good'! Jesus does not mean that he was not good. Jesus does not mean that he was not God!

- **Mark 10:21.** Jesus knows that this man is not as good as he thinks. So Jesus gives the man a **test**. This will show him his sin. It will show him that he loves his money and his position as a rich man. Jesus does not mean that the man is nearly perfect! Jesus does **not** mean that the man only had one thing wrong with him!

THE MAN'S PROBLEM
📖 *Mark 10:17-20*

The man's problem is not that he is too rich. His worst problem is that he thinks he is **so good**.

📖 *Mark 10:18.* See how Jesus questions the man. He does not know what 'good' means. The man thinks that he is **almost good enough** for God. He thinks that he has kept God's commands.

However, he is not sure. Perhaps he has missed something out. So he **runs** to Jesus and asks what else he must **do** to have eternal life.

> ⠕ *Many people think like this man. They talk about all the good things that they have done. If we think that we are almost good enough, we are a very long way from God.*
> *Remember* 📖 *Mark 10:14-15.*

JESUS' ANSWER
📖 *Mark 10:21-22*

Jesus knows that the man is only good **on the outside.** So he finds a way to show him what is wrong with him.

⊕ *Imagine! You are climbing a ladder or tree to reach something you want very much. You are nearly at the top. Then a friend shouts: 'You can only reach the top if you come down to the bottom!'. You would never believe him!*

The man is like that. He thinks that he is almost at the top. Jesus tells him: 'I will tell you how to reach heaven. You have to sell everything!' That will not take him up to the top! It will take him right down to the **bottom** of the ladder! He will become like a child. Then no one will think that he is important!

So he will never do that. However, **that is how to reach heaven.**

People thought that it was very important to be rich. They thought that if someone was rich, God must have blessed them. This man would never let go of all that and become last. 📖 *Mark 10:31.*

Summary: It **seems** as if Jesus tells the man the one last thing he needs to do to become perfect. **In fact**, Jesus shows the man how proud he is. **If we want to enter God's kingdom, we need to see our sin. We must not think we are good.**

> ⠕ *Are you ready to come down to the bottom of the ladder? Or are you still proud of all your good things?*
>
> *God gives eternal life to people who know that they have done nothing good. God gives eternal life to people who are humble and accept what he gives.*

41 ARE YOU WILLING TO BE LAST?

◉ Background

📖 *Mark 10:17-22.* The rich man needs to become like a little child to enter heaven.

📖 *Mark 10:32-34.* This is the third time Jesus tells the disciples that He is going to die. They must learn to follow Jesus down a road of pain. They must be willing to be last (Mark 8:31-38 and Mark 9:30-35).

📖 *Mark 10:23-31.*
Do you see how all this joins together?

◉ Main point

If you want to follow Jesus, you must be **ready to be last** – 📖 Mark 10:31.

✪ Something to work on

1. Always look for verses like Mark 10:31 that are like a key to open the chapter. Look back to **Mark 9:35.**

2. The disciples had left everything, but they were still like the rich man. They wanted to be first.

Are we like them too? In what ways can we have wrong thinking like this?

◉ Notes

• **Mark 10:25, 27.** Jesus' picture makes us laugh. It is impossible of course! A camel is like a big horse. People ride camels in the desert.

• **Mark 10:30.** What does Jesus' promise mean? He does not mean that Christians will become rich with money! If we give up our home for Jesus, he will not give us 100 actual houses. But many Christian homes will welcome us in! And Jesus blesses us in very many ways. We feel so rich when we have Jesus. 📖 *James 2:5, Philippians 3:7, 8.*

• **Mark 10:30.** 'Persecution.' This means that people will try to hurt us because we follow Jesus.

A CAMEL CANNOT GO THROUGH A NEEDLE

📖 *Mark 10:23-27*

Do you agree with Mark 10:25?

Of course Jesus is right. But **why** is it 'impossible' (Mark 10:27) for a rich man to be saved?

Remember the rich man in Mark 10:22. He loved **himself** more than he loved God. And he loved his **money** more than he loved God.

• What things do your listeners love more than they love God? Teach them that this stops them from being saved.

[As you teach them, remember Mark 10:27! Ask God to change people.]

PEOPLE WHO FOLLOW JESUS NEED TO BE LAST

📖 *Mark 10: 28-31*

In Mark 10:26, the disciples ask 'Who then can be saved?' Here is one answer: *people who do not think they are good or important!*

• So does Peter think that he **deserves** a place in God's kingdom? 📖 *Mark 10:28.*

Peter has not **earned** a place in heaven because he followed Jesus! He must not think like the rich man! 📖 *Mark 10:31.*

> 🔊 *Do you think that you have done very well for Jesus? You have done this... and this... surely you must be one of his best people! No! Who **does** Jesus put first? (Mark 10:31)*

• But did the disciples do **something good** when they followed Jesus? 📖 *Mark 10:28.*

Yes, they have done something good. 📖 *Mark 10:29, 30.* The disciples have left everything and followed Jesus. Jesus will look after anyone who trusts him like this. We deserve nothing, but Jesus is still pleased.

> 🔊 *Encourage the Christians! They may suffer a lot (Mark 10:30 promises trouble!), but Jesus will always care for them. They will gain more than they lose.*

Jesus does not mean that Christians will be rich and comfortable. We follow Jesus, who did not even have a home! *[Make sure your listeners understand this – see ⦿ Notes.]*

Think about all the good things Jesus has given Christians, and praise him!

42 WHY JESUS CAME

▣ Background

Soon Jesus will go to Jerusalem – to die. 📖 *Mark 10:32-34.*

The **disciples** still think that they will go to Jerusalem to rule! They imagine that they will become important people. They think that they will be rulers in Jesus' kingdom.

One more time, Jesus tells them the truth. He tells them that they need to become like him. They must be ready to be last, not to be first. 📖 *Mark 10:31.* They must be ready to serve, not to rule. 📖 *Mark 10:35-45.*

▣ Main point

Jesus came to **serve**, to die for his people. So they also must be willing to serve.

▣ Something to work on

There are two powerful messages in this section. We want to show **how wonderful Jesus is**, so that people will love and trust him. And we want **Christians to learn to serve**, like Jesus.

▣ Notes

- **Mark 10:38.** 'Drink the cup', 'baptism'. Jesus uses these pictures to speak about his **death**. He will drink the terrible cup of God's anger. He will be 'baptised' in the floods of God's judgement.

- **Mark 10:39-40.** The disciples give the wrong answer. Of course, they cannot suffer what Jesus has to. However, Jesus warns them that they will suffer! Jesus cannot promise them the best places, but he can promise them pain!

- **Mark 10:45.** This is the third time (in Mark) that Jesus says **why** he came. He came to **preach** the gospel (Mark 1:38). He came to call **sinners** (Mark 2:17). Now Jesus says that he came to **serve and die**.

- **Mark 10:45.** 'Ransom' or 'redeem'. You pay a 'ransom' when you pay money to set a slave free. Jesus came to set sinners free. He paid the price – his own blood.

JESUS CAME TO DIE
📖 *Mark 10:32-34, 45*

Imagine Mark 10:32! **Jesus** walks ahead. Jesus knows what will happen at Jerusalem, but he is ready. The **disciples** are behind Jesus. They are afraid; they do not want to go to Jerusalem.

So Jesus stops to talk to the disciples. He wants them to know that he **came to die**! When people kill Jesus, it is not a mistake. It is all God's plan. And Jesus will not die as a hero. He will die as a bad person.

> ⏵ *Jesus knows that people will spit on him. He knows that they will laugh at him and curse him. Even so, Jesus says yes to the cross. That is because the cross is the only way to save us. Do you love Jesus because he said yes to the cross? Will you say yes to the cross too? Will you follow this lovely Saviour, even when it is hard?*

JESUS CAME TO SERVE
📖 *Mark 10:45*

Kings do not serve, do they? Kings sit on high seats. Kings tell people to serve them!

That is what James and John thought. Jesus was King – and they wanted to sit next to him. They wanted to rule over others too (Mark 10:35-41).

But this King was different. King Jesus came **to serve.** He did not come for himself, he came for other people. He came to give his life for them. So Jesus has a lesson for all the disciples. 📖 *Mark 10:42-45.*

Jesus did not come to receive honour, but pain. Jesus did not come to have servants, but to serve. **Were his disciples willing to be like Jesus?**

> ⏵ *Jesus does not want us to be **important**. He wants us to **serve other people**. He does not want us to be **above** other people. He wants us to be **below** them. Do you love Jesus because he served you? So will you be a servant too? How will this show in your life?*

JESUS CAME TO GIVE
📖 *Mark 10:45*

Jesus came to give his life for people like us! He paid the price to set his people free! He died so that we could live! Do you love Jesus because he gave so much? So will you receive his free gift? Will you **receive** his love, his forgiveness, his life?

43 JESUS OPENS BLIND EYES

▣ Background

In Mark 8-10 Jesus teaches the disciples. He wants them to understand that he will die. They must not want to be important. They must be willing to suffer, because Jesus will suffer.

So why does Mark now tell us this story? 📖 *Mark 10:46-52.*

The blind man teaches the disciples an important lesson. The disciples still do not see why Jesus came. The blind man sees more than they do! He does not want to be important, like the disciples. He just wants Jesus to show him love! Think about Mark 10:15, 23.

◉ Main point

Jesus came to give. Will we receive?

✦ Something to work on

This talk is good for people who are not Christians. Tell everyone to invite their friends.

Remember that we all like to **do** something to make us good Christians! Help people to see that we only have to **ask** Jesus

something. Try to make the talk very easy, so that everyone can understand.

◉ Notes

• **Mark 10:46.** A blind man could not work, so he had to sit in the street and ask ('beg') for money. However, Bartimaeus knew that **Jesus** could give him something much better than money.

• **Mark 10:47.** Bartimaeus calls Jesus 'Son of David'. He understands that Jesus is the King (Messiah) who God has sent. He asks Jesus to have 'mercy' (pity) on him because he has great need and Jesus has great love.

A POOR BLIND MAN ASKS

📖 *Mark 10:46-50*

✚ *If you need something very much, who do you ask? You ask someone who is kind and will listen to you. You ask someone who can give you what you need.*

Bartimaeus knew that Jesus was the right person! He believed that Jesus was God's King. He believed that Jesus could make a blind man see. He believed that Jesus would listen. So he shouted! And he would not be quiet until Jesus answered him.

Jesus came to **give**. 📖 *Mark 10:45.* Jesus came to give his life for people like you and me. Jesus came to give us his love and forgiveness. He came to pay the price for our sins. *[Explain clearly who Jesus is. Tell the people why he came to die on the cross.* 📖 *Mark 10:33, 34.]*

> ➲ *If Jesus came to* **give**, *what do we have to do? Ask! We need to be like the blind man. We need to want Jesus very much. We need to cry out to Jesus until he answers us. We need to ask Jesus to show us his kindness.*

A POOR BLIND MAN RECEIVES

📖 *Mark 10:51-52*

Bartimaeus asked the right person! Jesus did not tell him to be quiet. Jesus did not say: 'I am not interested in a poor, dirty, blind man'. Instead, Jesus asked him this great question:

'What do you want me to do for you?'

Jesus never disappoints people who trust in him! The blind man sees! And what does he do then? 📖 *Mark 10:52.*

> ➲ *What do* **you** *want Jesus to do for you? Of course, Jesus* **can** *still heal us. But Jesus came to give us something far more important. Jesus came to* **give** *his life on the cross. Do you want to* **receive** *his gift of free forgiveness? And are you ready to follow Jesus, like the blind man? Then ask, and you will receive, like the blind man!* 📖 *Matthew 7:7-8.*

[You may like to talk about 📖 *Mark 10:36, 37. That time Jesus did* **not** *give what James and John asked for. What is the wrong kind of thing to ask?]*

44 THE KING COMES!

◉ Background

The second half of Mark is about **why Jesus came**. In Mark 8-10, Jesus **talked** a lot to the disciples. He told them that he had come to die.

Now it is time for **action**. In Mark 11, Jesus enters Jerusalem one week before he will die on the cross. The people have a last opportunity to believe in their King. However, they will refuse him and kill him.

In Mark 11, the people **welcome** Jesus. He is the King who God has promised. They are very excited. They think that the time has come. At last, they will have a King in Jerusalem! 📖 *Mark 11:1-11.*

◉ Main point

Jesus **is** God's King. But is he the King that we want?

✳ Something to work on

It is very easy to be like the crowds. It is easy to sing praise to Jesus, and say that we are Christians. However, many people do not really want Jesus to be their King. They want a hero, not a Saviour. They want someone to help them, not a King to serve. They want to feel good. They do not want people to hate them. They do not want a King who comes on a donkey and goes to the cross.

◉ Notes

• **Mark 11:2.** The 'colt' was a young donkey. A donkey is smaller than a horse. Ordinary people sometimes rode on a donkey. But kings rode on horses! Jesus is a different kind of King. He is a King on a donkey. He is a humble King who brings peace. He is the kind of king that God said he would send; 📖 *Zechariah 9:9-10.*

• **Mark 11:8.** They did this to welcome Jesus as their King.

• **Mark 11:9, 10.** 'Hosanna' means 'save' or 'praise'. The people use the words of a psalm about God's Messiah (King). 📖 *Psalm 118:25, 26.* They see that Jesus is God's King. They praise God. They want God's King to come and save them.

THE KING NEEDS A DONKEY

📖 *Mark 11:1-6*

Jesus needs a donkey. He is going to ride into Jerusalem. He wants the people to say that he is God's King. Until now, Jesus has not wanted to attract crowds of people. Now it is time for the people to say who he is. Many people are on their way to Jerusalem, because it is a special time (Passover). These people will welcome Jesus as King.

So Jesus needs a donkey to ride on. He does not want a horse. He wants a young donkey. In the Old Testament, the prophet Zechariah said that God's King will come on a donkey. God's King is a humble King. He has not come for war. He has come to bring peace.

The King needs a donkey. Notice that the King knows where to find the donkey. And the King has the right to tell people to let him take the donkey. King Jesus is in complete control as he goes towards his death!

> ⏩ *Jesus is certainly God's King! He makes everything happen as God said in the Old Testament. But do you want a King who is humble like Jesus?*

WELCOME THE KING WHO RIDES A DONKEY

📖 *Mark 11:7-11*

The crowds are so excited. They throw their clothes on the ground for Jesus. They cut branches from trees to welcome the King. They shout and sing. They praise God for Jesus. At last, God has sent the King to save them.

They are right! Everyone should praise God for King Jesus. He is the Saviour who God has sent. We all need Jesus so badly.

However, do they really want a King who rides on a donkey? We know that a week later the King of the Jews will die on the cross. Now they praise Jesus – soon they will kill him. He is God's King but they do not want him. He is not the kind of hero King that they want to follow.

> ⏩ *Think carefully about what you know about Jesus. [Talk about what we have learned from Mark.] Is Jesus really the kind of king that you are willing to follow?*

> ⏩ *It is right to sing songs about Jesus. It is good to praise Jesus, and say that he is King. But will you truly welcome Jesus as King over your life? Will you follow the King who rides on a donkey and goes to the cross?*

45 THE KING COMES TO HIS TEMPLE

◉ Background

The people have welcomed King Jesus into Jerusalem. They have praised God. God has sent their Saviour. 📖 *Mark 11:1-11.*

God's King is not only the Saviour. He is also the Judge. When God's King comes to God's temple, what will he find? And what will he do? 📖 *Mark 11:12-19; Malachi 3:1-2.*

◉ Main point

King Jesus is not happy when we pretend to follow him. He wants to see 'fruit', real faith and love.

◉ Notes

• **Mark 11:11.** 'Temple.' God told the Jews to worship him there. There they must kill animals as 'sacrifices' to God. The temple in Jerusalem was the centre of their worship.

• **Mark 11:13-14.** Jesus sees the fig tree as a **picture of the temple worship.** The tree had lots of leaves, but no fruit. It looked good, but it was no good. Jesus judges the tree (Mark 11:14). He does this to show that he will judge the temple.

• **Mark 11:15.** Jesus is perfect. He never sinned when he was angry. Jesus was right to be angry. The King came to his temple and found it full of sin.

• **Mark 11:15, 16.** It was a special time for the Jews, called 'Passover'. They came to the temple to sacrifice animals to God. It was not wrong to change their money so they could buy an animal. But they were using the temple to cheat people and get rich! They did not care about God. They wanted to make money for themselves.

• **Mark 11:17.** The main problem is not that people cheated each other. The Jews robbed **God.** They only pretended to worship him in his house. Really, they cared about themselves.

A TREE WITH NO FRUIT
📖 *Mark 11:11-14*

> ➤ *If Jesus walked into our meeting today, what would Jesus want to find?*
>
> *Would Jesus look at things on the **outside**? How many meetings we have? How nice our clothes are? How loudly we sing?*
>
> *Or would Jesus look **inside** us? For love and faith and holy lives? The Bible calls these inside things **fruit**.*

King Jesus walks towards his temple in Jerusalem. Will he find that God's people love and worship God there? Will he find fruit?

On his way, Jesus sees something. He sees a fig tree. It is full of leaves, but it has no fruit. It looks good, but it is no good to eat. It is like what happens at the temple!

Jesus curses the fig tree. 📖 ***Mark 11:14.*** This also has a message about the temple. Jesus will judge the false worship of many Jews.

> ➤ *Jesus **does** come to our meetings! What fruit does he find in your life? Is Jesus sad and angry because it is all on the outside?*

A TEMPLE WITH NO WORSHIP
📖 *Mark 11:15-19*

• What does King Jesus want to find when he comes to his temple?

• What does he find?

It is all on the outside! They pretend to worship God. They sacrifice the animals to God. They make Passover a special time for God. It all looks good. But Jesus sees that there is no real fruit. There is no love, no real prayer, no true worship.

King Jesus is right to be angry. The King will not accept false worship in his temple.

So what do the leaders think about what Jesus did? Are they sorry for what they have done wrong – or do they hate God's King? 📖 *Mark 11:18.*

> ➤ *Jesus is the Saviour from God. He is also the **Judge** from God. Jesus looks for fruit in our lives. Jesus is angry with us when we only look like Christians on the outside. Will you ask Jesus to forgive you and change your heart?*

46 HAVE FAITH IN GOD!

◉ Background

Jesus has just shown his great power. He has the right to judge the temple. He is in control.
📖 *Mark 11:15-19.*

Next day, when Peter sees the dead fig tree, he is very surprised. Jesus has again shown his great power.
📖 *Mark 11:20-21.*

Jesus wants the disciples to know where this power has come from. Soon, he will go from them, but they can put faith in God's power.
📖 *Mark 11:22-25.*

◉ Main point

Have faith in God. Then anything is possible.

✶ Something to work on

We must try not to make these two mistakes.

1. God does not promise to give us whatever we **decide to ask for**! Jesus says: 'Have faith in God'. God does not do things that are not his will! He will not give us things that are not good for us! Think about 📖 1 John 5:14-15; 1 John 3:22; John 15:7. When we want God's will, then nothing is too difficult for God to give us.

2. We must not think that this promise is not for us! It is not just for special people. Jesus says that **anyone** can ask. We do not need big faith, because we have a big God. We only have to trust that God means what he says.
📖 Matthew 17:20-21.

◉ Notes

• **Mark 11:20.** In one day, the fig tree became dry and died. Jesus has God's power to judge.

• **Mark 11:25.** Notice how important it is to **forgive** other people. Remember how much God has forgiven us. God will not hear our prayers if we will not forgive other people.

HAVE FAITH IN GOD!

📖 *Mark 11:22*

Soon Jesus will go from the disciples. He will not be there to do great miracles. And they will face many big problems. How will they feel?

Have faith in God! Jesus wants them to know that God's power is there for them. They must learn to trust God. Now they follow Jesus, and ask Jesus for what they need. Soon they must live by faith in **God**, and ask him for all they need.

• Often, we do not really have faith in God. Why is this?

• Why is it safe to trust in God? What is God like?

NOTHING IS TOO HARD FOR GOD!

📖 *Mark 11:23-24*

[⊞ Tell a story about this. Tell a story about someone who you heard about. Or, tell a story from the Bible. For example, Elijah. 📖 James 5:17-18; 1 Kings 17:1, 18:41-45.]

Many things are too hard for us. We see a big problem. We know that we cannot do something. So we become sad. We give up. Often we forget that God can do it! If it is God's will,

we can ask God, and he will do it!

• Does Jesus say that we can only ask God for things that are a little bit too hard for us? Does it matter how impossible it is? Why?

Of course, Jesus does not want us to move real mountains! He uses a picture to help us see that nothing is too hard for God! No problem is a problem to God.

> ⯈ *When you have a problem, what will you do? Will you worry? Or get upset? Or give up? Or will you* ***have faith in God?***

ASK AND RECEIVE!

📖 *Mark 11:23-24*

Often we do not know what God's will is. We must trust God to do whatever is right. Sometimes we do know what God's will is. So we can believe that God **will** answer. When we have faith in God, he answers!

⊞ It was nearly time for the speaker to preach. The wind blew so loudly that no one could hear. The man remembered this promise. He knew that it was God's will for the people to hear. So he asked the wind to stop. He believed it would. As he stood up to preach, the wind was silent. When he finished, the wind started again!

107

47 WHAT RIGHT DO YOU HAVE TO DO THIS?

◾ Background

The leaders of the Jews are angry. They have control over the people. If people believe in Jesus, these leaders will lose their control.

The leaders are angry because the crowds welcomed Jesus as their King. 📖 *Mark 11:8-10.*

The leaders are angry because Jesus threw the people out of the temple. 📖 *Mark 11:15-17.*

Now they look for a way to kill Jesus. 📖 *Mark 11:18.*

So they ask Jesus a question. But they do not really want to know the true answer. They only want to get Jesus into trouble. If Jesus says that he is King, they can tell the Romans. The Romans control the country. Caesar is king! No one else can claim to be king!

📖 *Mark 11:27-33.*

⊙ Main point

We know that Jesus does have the right to do as he wants. Jesus is the King who should rule over our lives.

✶ Something to work on

It is easy to **say** that we want Jesus to rule our lives. But do we really want him to? Even in Jesus' church, we can want to do things **our** way! What things do your listeners find hard to give over to Jesus?

◾ Notes

- **Mark 11:29.** Jesus will always answer an honest question. This time, Jesus knows that it is best not to answer. It is best to show these people that they are not honest. If they answer his question, they will know the answer to their own question!

A QUESTION FROM THE JEWS

📖 *Mark 11:27-28*

⊞ *Imagine a little boy. He is very angry with a big strong man. He hits the man as hard as he can. Suddenly, the boy is on the ground. He has not even hurt the man. The boy feels very silly.*

The leaders of the Jews are like the little boy. They hate Jesus. They want their question to hurt him. But Jesus is far too strong. At the end, they feel silly.

• They want to hear Jesus answer the question. But they know the answer already. What is it?

Jesus has the right to do these things because **God** has sent him. God has sent his Son to be King. The temple belongs to him.

But they do not want God's King. **They** want control over the people and over the temple. So they hate Jesus.

> ⨠ *Who has the right to rule your life? Who has the right to tell you how to live? You know the answer. Jesus has that right. God says so.*

> ⨠ *But do you want to control your own life? Do you fight against what Jesus says?*

A QUESTION FROM JESUS

📖 *Mark 11:29-33*

Jesus does not answer their question. Instead, he asks them a question! It is not just any question. It hits them very hard and wins the fight!

• Why is Jesus' question such a good one? 📖 *Mark 11:29-32.*

Everyone knew that John was a prophet from God. So they should believe what John says. And John told people that Jesus is the King from God! So, if John is from God, then Jesus is from God too!

If these Jews give an honest answer to Jesus, then they answer their own question! So they say that they do not know. That is a lie! They know the answer to Jesus' question. But they do not want to say it.

> ⨠ *Some people do not want to follow Jesus. They ask questions, but they do not want to know the truth. They answer questions, but they do not tell the truth. They do not want King Jesus to rule over their lives. Are you like that?*

48 WHERE IS THE FRUIT?

◉ Background

The leaders of the Jews want to kill Jesus. They want Jesus to say something which they can report to Herod, the Roman ruler. 📖 **Mark 11:27-28; Mark 12:13-15.**

Jesus wants to show these leaders their sin. Jesus is the Messiah from God. But they want to kill the King who God has sent! 📖 **Mark 11:17-18; Mark 12:1-12.**

This story answers the question in **Mark 11:28.** God's Son has the right to do these things!

◉ Main point

God has sent his Son to find fruit. But they kill him.

◉ Notes

• **Mark 12:1.** A 'vineyard' is where people grow vines. Vines produce fruit called grapes, which make wine.

• **Mark 12:1.** 'tenants.' These are the farmers in the story. They grow the vines. Tenants do not own the farmland. They look after it for the owner.

• **Mark 12:1.** The story comes from

Isaiah 5:1-7. Israel is the 'vineyard' in the story. God has done everything possible for his people. But there is no good fruit. Instead, Israel produces bad fruit.

Jesus changes the story a little. In his story, he tells *farmers* ('tenants') to look after his vineyard. These tenants stand for the *leaders* of the Jews. When God sends his *servants* (the prophets) to look for fruit, the tenants (leaders) attack them. (The last prophet was John the Baptist. Did the leaders of the Jews listen to him?) At last, God sends his *Son*. But the leaders want to keep the fruit. They are thieves (📖 **Mark 11:17**). They want to keep control of the people. So they kill God's Son.

• **Mark 12:7.** 'Heir.' The owner's son. The vineyard (farm) will belong to the son. So they kill the son to have the farm ('inheritance') for themselves.

• **Mark 12:10.** Jesus uses these words from **Psalm 118:22, 23.** The psalm tells what the Jews will do to their Messiah. They 'reject' (throw away) the most important stone in the building (God's church). That stone is Jesus!

GOD HAS SENT HIS SON
📖 *Mark 12:6-8*

[Think how to tell the story (or act it out), so that everyone understands it. Make sure that your listeners understand what Jesus means by his story. The owner = God. The farmers (tenants) = leaders of the Jews. The servants = prophets. The son = Jesus.]

In the story, the owner sent many servants first. However, the farmers would not listen to the servants. The owner did not give up. At last, the owner sent his own son. He said: 'Surely they will respect my son!'

• How much did the owner want to have his fruit?

• Why did God send his Son?

God sent Jesus for a very important reason. Jesus came to be the King from God! Jesus came to demand what belongs to him! He said, 'Give me my fruit! Give me my people!'

And the leaders said: 'No! We want the fruit. Let us kill God's Son.'

⧉ *What will **we** do with God's Son?*

*Remember, **God** has sent him! It is very important. He demands fruit from us. He tells us to turn away from our sin and believe in him (Mark 1:15). Do you say: 'No, go away?' Do you say: 'I am too busy now'? Will you say no to God's own Son?*

WHAT WILL GOD DO?
📖 *Mark 12:9*

Will God say, 'I do not mind if they kill my Son?' Will God say, 'Let them have my fruit if they want it'? Will God say, 'They can choose what they do with my Son?'

Of course not! God is angry. God will punish the people who do not want his Son. God will judge those who will not give him his fruit.

(Jesus will be the most important stone in God's new temple, his church. This is what the Old Testament said.
📖 *Mark 12:10-11.*

⧉ *What will God do to us, if we say no to God's Son? Remember that he has risen from the dead and he is King. Our lives should belong to him. He will judge us if we steal the fruit for ourselves.*

49 GIVE TO GOD WHAT BELONGS TO GOD

▣ Background

See ▣ **Background** for Mark 12:1-12.

Remember this. Everything we have read in Mark 11-12 happened in the last week of Jesus' life. At the end of the week, they will kill Jesus. However, Mark 12 shows that Jesus is in control. They can only kill Jesus when he gives himself up to them!

▣ Main point

Give to God what belongs to God.

▣ Something to work on

Many Christians do not understand that they belong **completely** to God. They give God a little money, a little time. And they please themselves with the rest.

📖 *1 Corinthians 6:19-20; Romans 6:13.*

▣ Notes

• **Mark 12:13.** The 'Pharisees' are Jews who love their religion. The 'Herod' group do not care about God or religion. Both groups hate Jesus. They come together to kill him. 📖 *Mark 3:6.*

• **Mark 12:14-15.** They pretend to say nice things about Jesus. They want Jesus to think that they respect him. Jesus knows what they really want. They want to get him in trouble. They want to use Jesus' answer against him.

• **Mark 12:15.** It is a clever question. If Jesus says yes, the ordinary Jews will turn against him. If Jesus says 'no', he will be in trouble with Herod, the Roman ruler.

• **Mark 12:16.** Every coin of Roman money ('denarius') had a picture of Caesar's face on it. Caesar ('the emperor') was king over a large part of the world (the 'Roman empire'). The money even belonged to Caesar!

GIVE TO CAESAR!

📖 *Mark 12:13-17*

[Explain this. The two groups come together to get Jesus into trouble. Show how clever the question is. Then talk about Jesus' wise answer.]

'Show me a Roman coin!' The Romans ruled over the Jews and the Jews hated it. The Jews thought that God's people should not have to pay taxes to Caesar!

However, they all used Roman coins. Jesus asks them to show him one. And on every Roman coin was the face of Caesar. The coin belonged to him. So if Caesar wants them to pay taxes, they must pay!

> ⧆ *You probably have to pay taxes to the government too. Perhaps the government does evil things, like Caesar did. Jesus wants us to pay taxes! So do not complain – and do not try to cheat!*
> 📖 **Romans 13:1-7.**

GIVE TO GOD!

📖 *Mark 12:17*

Their question is clever. But Jesus' answer was better! Both groups know that what Jesus says is true. They must give taxes to Caesar because it belongs to him. And they must give to God what belongs to God!

⊕ *We are like coins. We all show the image of God. He made us. We belong to him. Therefore, we must give him whatever he asks for!*

• **What does God ask from us?**
   (📖 **Mark 12:29-31**)

God sends his own Son to say 'Give to God what belongs to God'. However, these people will not listen. They do not really love God. They do not want to give up their lives to God. So they try to kill God's Son.

> ⧆ *Jesus says to **us**: 'Give to God what belongs to God'. Are you glad to do that? Do you say: 'My money is God's money, my time is God's time, my life is all for God'?*

> ⧆ *We have all robbed God. We have lived for ourselves. Remember, Jesus came to pay all our debts on the cross. He came to forgive us. And he came to claim our lives, to have us back. What do you need to give back to God?*

50 A BAD MISTAKE

▣ Background

Different groups of Jews come to Jesus to ask questions. They do not want to know the answers. They are hard questions. They think that Jesus will not be able to answer them. They want to trap Jesus. They want to make Jesus look silly. In the end, they want to kill him.

The next group to test Jesus is the Sadducees. 📖 *Mark 12:18-27.*

⊡ Main point

Do not make a bad mistake! Believe what the Bible says!

✳ Something to work on

It is easy to make the same bad mistake as the Sadducees. We can hold on too strongly to what others say, or to what our traditions say. Or we can listen too quickly to new teaching. The teaching may attract us. It may promise good things. Then we may not look carefully at what **God** says in the Bible. We may not want to believe what the Bible says. We become blind.

▣ Notes

• **Mark 12:18.** The **Sadducees** were very different from the Pharisees. They only believed in the first five books of the Old Testament, which Moses wrote. They did not believe that people will rise from death.

• **Mark 12:20.** The Sadducees make up a story. They do not believe in a resurrection day (when our dead bodies will be given new life). They think that their story makes resurrection look silly. A woman marries seven times to brothers who die, one after another. This is what the Old Testament says to do. So, when they all rise from death, who will she be married to? They think that this is too hard for Jesus to answer!

• **Mark 12:26-27.** (📖 *Exodus 3:6*). God made great promises to Abraham, Isaac and Jacob. They never received what God promised while they were alive on earth. But God keeps his promises! God is still the God of Abraham, Isaac and Jacob. They are not dead and finished. Their spirits are alive. They wait for resurrection day. Their bodies will rise from the dead. Then they will receive the promises which they believed.

A QUESTION ABOUT RESURRECTION
📖 *Mark 12:23*

The Sadducees want to make Jesus look silly. *[Explain the story that the Sadducees told. Explain why they thought that it was a problem for Jesus.]*

It was easy for Jesus to answer.
📖 *Mark 12:25.* In heaven, we will have real bodies. But they will not be the same as our bodies on earth. In heaven, we will have real friends. However, it will not be the same as on earth. We will not marry, or have children!
📖 *1 Corinthians 15:35-44.*

> ⏩ *It is very important to believe that one day our bodies will rise from death. We will have real bodies, better bodies. If we believe in Jesus, we will live with him forever. We may have many questions about it. What will it be like? Do not worry. Believe what God tells us in the Bible.*

Jesus shows the Sadducees what the Old Testament teaches. It says that we will rise from death. The Sadducees only believed the parts of the Bible that Moses wrote. Jesus teaches them from a book that Moses wrote – Exodus. He shows that God is a God for living people, not for dead people! God is still our God after we die in this life. This is because we are not finished. Our bodies will rise to life. *[Explain Mark 12:26-27 – see* ◉ **Notes***]*

A QUESTION ABOUT US
📖 *Mark 12:24, 27*

Have we made a bad mistake like the Sadducees?

Choose which one is the problem with the Sadducees:

• Did they find the Bible hard to understand?

• Or did they not **want** to believe the Bible?

God loves to help us when we find it hard to understand the Bible. Ask God to help you. Ask your teachers to help you.

However, the Sadducees were wrong because they did not want to believe. They did not accept the Bible's teaching. They did not **like** what the Bible says. That is why they did 'not know the Scriptures or the power of God.' Jesus says: 'This is a bad mistake. How wrong you are!'

> ⏩ *Are you willing to believe* **everything** *God says in the Bible? If you do not like something, what do you do? Do you ask God to help you accept it? [Talk more about this.] Do not make this bad mistake!*

51 LOVE THE LORD YOUR GOD WITH ALL YOUR HEART!

▣ Background

Jesus is in Jerusalem. It is the last week before he dies. Many Jews want to kill him. However, they do not know how to do this. They ask clever questions to get Jesus into trouble.

Now, someone else comes to Jesus with a question! It will be the last one. Jesus gives such good answers. So no one is willing to ask any more questions.

This man is different. He does not hate Jesus. He wants to learn. He truly wants to know the answer to his question. 📖 *Mark 12:28-34.*

◉ Main point

Receive God's truth like this man! Understand that **love** is the way to keep God's commands.

✴ Something to work on

Rules are quite easy to keep. But God wants **all our love!** This is impossible for us! Think how to show your listeners this.

◉ Notes

- **Mark 12:28.** Most of the **'teachers of the law'** were against Jesus. Their job was to study and teach God's laws. They taught hundreds of little laws which are not in the Bible. They told people to keep all these little laws as well as God's commands.

- **Mark 12:28-30.** Remember, the teachers of the law taught **hundreds** of laws. So which one is the most important? Jesus does not give a **new** answer. He says the words of Deuteronomy 6:4-6. The teachers of the law knew these words well. They are important words in the Old Testament.

- **Mark 12:31.** Jesus adds a second command. This one is from Leviticus 19:18. Jesus knows that if you love God, you will also love other people. The two things belong together. They also sum up the Ten Commandments.

- **Mark 12:34.** The man is 'not far from the kingdom of God'. This is because he sees an important truth. We must keep God's laws in our **hearts**. Of course, he cannot do this! Now he needs to believe in Jesus.

A MAN WHO WANTS TO KNOW
📖 *Mark 12:28*

There are two kinds of people. Some people want to get away from God's truth and some people want to know it. Some people push God's truth away and some people receive it. Which one are you?

This teacher of the law (Mark 12:28) wants to know God's truth! Other people have come to ask Jesus hard questions. But this man is different. He knows that Jesus can help him to find the truth.

What happens when Jesus gives him a very hard answer? 📖 *Mark 12:32-33.* The man does not say, 'It is too difficult'. He does not have excuses. He **receives** Jesus' answer. He knows that Jesus is right. The man knows that he needs to keep this command.

> ⏩ *What do you say when God's word is hard? 'I cannot do that!' 'I am better than other people are!' 'God does not really mean it!' [Talk about more excuses.]*

A LAW THAT WE NEED TO KEEP
📖 *Mark 12:32-33*

> ⊕ *A man has two sons. He gives one son a hundred laws to keep. He tells the other son only to love him. Both sons do what their father says. Which son pleases the father most?*

This teacher of the law taught hundreds of little rules. Now he sees that God really wants one thing. God wants our love – not lots of sacrifices.

We can give all our money to God. We can go to church every day. We can pray all week. But these things are nothing without love.

> ⏩ *How much love does God want?*

> ⏩ *How well have you kept this command? How easy is it?*

This man saw the truth – do you? God tells us to love him, and other people, with all our heart. But we cannot do it! We cannot begin to do it. We love ourselves too much. So we are in trouble with God.

> ⏩ *This is why we need **Jesus**. He came to forgive people who have **failed** to love God. Jesus was on his way to the cross, to die for our sins. Ask Jesus to be your Saviour!*

52 TAKE OR GIVE?

◉ Background

Different people have come to Jesus to ask difficult questions. They want to get him into trouble and kill him. Now it is Jesus' turn to ask them a difficult question!

Jesus wants to show the people that these teachers are wrong. They are wrong about Jesus. They are also wrong in the way they live. They **take** things for themselves. They do not care about other people, or even God.

It is much better to be like the poor widow. She wanted to **give** everything.

📖 *Mark 12:35-44*

◉ Main point

Watch out for bad teachers, who want things for themselves. Be like the widow who truly loved God and gave everything.

✱ Something to work on

The widow in Mark 12:41-44 is a powerful example. But be careful! The main point is not to make people give more money. Jesus notices the person who gave a tiny bit! Jesus teaches here about a giving **heart**.

◉ Notes

• **Mark 12:35-37.** When Jesus came to Jerusalem last Sunday, the people sang 'Hosanna to the Son of David'. The teachers of the law were angry. They did not want people to call Jesus 'Son of David'. That means Jesus is 'the Christ' or 'Messiah'.

• Now Jesus teaches them what their scriptures say about 'the Christ'. He is even more important than they thought. The Christ is not just a man, because David calls him 'Lord'. So these teachers of the law should call Jesus something even better than 'Son of David'! They should honour him as Lord and God!

• **Mark 12:40.** The teachers of the law look very holy. The truth is that they are greedy and cruel. They take money from widows who need help. We do not really know what they did, but Jesus thinks that it is stealing!

DANGER! BAD TEACHERS!
📖 *Mark 12:35-40*

- A teacher may tell good stories. He may make us laugh. He may have come from a big church. But how can we tell if he is a bad teacher?

1. He does not teach all the truth.
📖 *Mark 12:35-37.*

[Explain these verses – see ⊙ *Notes].* The teachers of the law did not want to accept what the Bible says! They made the Bible say the things that they wanted to say.

> ⨠ *Do not accept teachers who do not want to follow God's word. They (and we) must be willing for the Bible to change us.*

2. A bad teacher only cares about himself. 📖 *Mark 12:38-40.*

The teachers of the law looked very good. They prayed a lot. They were at all the important meetings. They wanted everyone to know how good they were. **However, it was all for themselves.** They were greedy. They wanted power. They wanted money. And they did not care about people in need, like widows.

> ⨠ *Some Christian leaders are like this. Be very careful! We all like to listen to a famous teacher. But does he want to honour God? Or does he want money? Does he want everyone to think how good he is?*

> ⨠ *What will happen to people like this?* 📖 *Mark 12:40.*

GOOD EXAMPLE! SOMEONE WHO GIVES EVERYTHING!
📖 *Mark 12:41-44*

- How is this widow different from the teachers of the law?

> ⊕ *God had saved many people in this place. Everyone wanted to hear the preacher. Someone asked him, 'Why do you have so much success?' The preacher said 'Look over there and you will see.' An old woman went slowly past, into the church. 'She comes every day to pray.'*

That woman was like the widow in Mark 12. She gave everything. The widow gave all her money. This woman gave all her time to God. She did not want anyone to notice her. She loved God. So she loved to give.

> ⨠ *Jesus knows who really loves him. Other people notice the great preachers. But Jesus sees the person who loves to give.*

53 EXPECT TROUBLE

◉ Background

At the end of the week, Jesus will die on the cross. Then he will return to heaven. Jesus knows that many painful things will happen in the world. His friends must know that these are not a mistake. Jesus promises that these hard things will happen. They must trust Jesus. They must wait for Jesus to come back to judge the world. 📖 **Mark 13.**

◉ Main point

Be ready for trouble. Do not let go of God's truth. Trust that Jesus is in control.

✱ Things to work on

1. Mark 13 is difficult to understand. Matthew 24 may help you. Bible teachers explain some parts in different ways. We must study carefully. Then we must ask God to help us teach **the main things clearly.** We do not want to confuse our people. Jesus has some very important messages for us. Pray that we will all listen to these clear messages.

2. Jesus talks about two different events in this chapter. **1) God's judgment on Jerusalem.** The Romans will destroy the temple and all Jerusalem in the year 70 (70 years after Jesus was born). **2) The end of the world**, when Jesus will come to judge the whole world.

Sometimes, in Mark 13, it is not clear which one Jesus means. The two events are similar. God's judgement on Jerusalem is a picture of God's judgement on the world. Jesus wants his people to be ready for both.

◉ Notes

• **Mark 13:4.** 📖 *Matthew 24:3.* The disciples think that the temple will be destroyed at the end of the world, when Jesus comes back. So Jesus' answer is about both events 1) and 2).

• **Mark 13:7-8.** When big trouble happens in the world, some people think that it is the end of the world. Jesus tells us this is wrong! It is like when you have a baby. The first pains tell you that you must be ready! But it will be a long time before the baby comes out. Wars and disasters tell us to be ready for the end of the world. But they do **not** mean that the end has come.

TROUBLE WILL COME!

📖 *Mark 13:2, 7*

⊕ *Do you have a nice strong church building that will last for many years? Perhaps you helped build it. You are proud of it. Then someone says: 'Soon it will be a pile of broken pieces!' What would you think?*

The Jews thought that their temple was the most important building. The temple was the centre of all their worship. And it was so big and so beautiful! The stones were strong and it should last for ever. Now Jesus says that it will all be gone. This seems very bad, terrible!

Jesus wants us to be ready for terrible things.

> ⏩ *What terrible things have happened in your country or village?*
>
> ⏩ *What are you afraid may happen?*
>
> *Remember that Jesus says that trouble will come. The temple will not be there, but Jesus' plan is still there. Someone may burn down your church building, but Jesus is still in control! Wars and earthquakes, floods and famine will all happen. Jesus has said so. None of these things changes the truth about Jesus. Do not think that God's plan has gone wrong. Trust him.*

DO NOT LET GO OF GOD!

📖 *Mark 13:7*

Of course trouble makes us feel sad! But Jesus does not want us to **go wrong** when trouble happens.

⊕ *Imagine someone asks you to hold something. He tells you that it will get hot, but **do not let go!** If you let go, it will break. Jesus tells us that painful things will happen, but do not let go of the truth! Do not go wrong!*

When big trouble happens, Jesus tells us two things we must not do.

1. We must not think that the end of the world has come (Mark 13:7).

> ⏩ *[The ● **Notes** will help you explain this.] Jesus wants us to **carry on** with our Christian lives. Terrible things will happen, but they do **not** mean that the end of the world has come. Keep calm. Pray. See how you can help.*

2. We must not believe wrong teaching (Mark 13:5).

> ⏩ *Always ask this question – 'Is this what the Bible says?' Some people will say strange and exciting things. Jesus warns us that they will 'deceive' many people (many people will believe their lies). Only believe what the Bible says!*

54 KEEP ON TELLING THE GOOD NEWS

▣ Background

Jesus wants to prepare his disciples for the future. After Jesus has gone, they will face a lot of trouble. They must not think that the end has come. People will hate them. They will say: 'Keep quiet about Jesus!' However, the disciples must be ready to keep speaking out about Jesus.

- **What things does Jesus want us to do when trouble comes?**
  📖 *Mark 13:9-13.*

◉ Main point

We must tell the good news to everyone. Do not let anyone stop you!

✧ Something to work on

Your listeners may face real danger, just as it says here. Help them not to hide their faith. Pray that this section will give them courage.

Or, it may be easy for your listeners to say that they believe in Jesus. Help them to care for Christians in other places who do suffer for Jesus. How can they find out? How can they help?

◉ Notes

- **Mark 13:10.** The disciples expected Jesus to come back very soon. However, before Jesus returns, God's people have work to do. All the different groups of people around the world need to hear the good news.

- **Mark 13:11. Usually** God wants us to think carefully before we speak. We must not think that the first thing that we think of is from God! However, here Jesus promises **special** help in times of great trouble ('when you are arrested'). When we stand up for him, he will certainly help us. We do not need to worry.

- **Mark 13:13.** Christians can say that Jesus **has already** saved them at the cross. That means we are safe, because we trust in Jesus. However, Jesus also says that we need to keep on to the end. Then we will be saved. Salvation is like a journey that begins at the cross and ends in heaven. People who trust in Jesus need to trust him until the end of their lives. Then they will go to be with Jesus.

PEOPLE WILL HATE YOU
📖 *Mark 13:9, 12, 13*

We want everyone to love us! We want people to think that we are good people! We never want to make them hate us! So we try not to say things that they will not like.
• *But what does Jesus say?*

Many Christians have found a way to avoid difficulty. They talk about Jesus with their Christian friends. But they do not tell other people that they are Christians. They keep quiet about Jesus. Then people will not hate them.
• *But what does Jesus say?*

› *How much do you love Jesus? If someone wants to beat you, will you say that you love Jesus? If your family will hate you, will you still love Jesus?*

› *This is so hard! Ask Jesus to help you!*

WHAT JESUS TELLS US TO DO

1. EVERYONE MUST HEAR ABOUT JESUS!
📖 *Mark 13:10*

We must not let anyone stop us. We may be afraid, but everyone must hear about Jesus. This is Jesus' plan. Even when rulers or police try to stop us, they too need to hear about Jesus (Mark 13:9).

› *Who can you or your church tell about Jesus? Think of people who do not hear about Jesus.*

2. DO NOT WORRY!
📖 *Mark 13:11*

Jesus will look after us when we suffer for him! He has promised to give us the right words to say. Jesus does not want us to worry. He wants us to speak out. Trust him!

3. KEEP ON TO THE END!
📖 *Mark 13:13*

It is hard, but do not give up! Jesus will help you through to the end.
[⊞ You could use a word picture of a journey with many difficulties.]

› *What things make you feel like giving up?*

› *How do Jesus' words give you courage and strength to keep going?*

55 DO NOT BELIEVE EVERYTHING!

◉ Background

Before Jesus returns, there will be a time of very great trouble. Jesus wants to prepare us for this.

Also, in the year AD 70, there would be a time of very great trouble. Jesus wanted to prepare his disciples for this. This happened in their lifetime.

This section describes both of these times. God's judgement of Jerusalem 70 years after Jesus was born is a picture. It is like God's judgement of the world, when Jesus returns.

📖 *Mark 13:14-27*. What things does Jesus warn of?

◉ Main point

There will be a time of great trouble before Jesus returns.

Do not believe everything you hear about the end of the world!

✦ Something to work on

When we talk about the end of the world, some people are very excited. They have many ideas about what may happen. Then they can miss what **Jesus** wants us to learn! In your talk, be careful to keep to what the Bible says. Keep to Jesus' main point. He wants us to be **ready** when great trouble comes.

◉ Notes

• **Mark 13:14.** Daniel talks about this terrible event in the temple (Daniel 11:31). A foreign king will come to worship idols in God's temple. When this happens, Christians in Jerusalem must run for their lives!

• **Mark 13:15-18.** This section is about what would happen in Jerusalem in the year 70. This would be in 40 years from then. The Roman army would come to destroy the temple. This was **God's** judgement. (The Jews did not believe in their Messiah. Instead, they kept to their old religion.) However, God did not want to judge the **Christians** in Jerusalem! So Jesus told them to run away fast!

• **Mark 13:19-20.** Jesus is probably talking about what will happen just before the **end of the world**. This is what he speaks of next (Mark 13:24; Matthew 24:29 – 'immediately after…')

A TERRIBLE TIME OF TROUBLE
📖 *Mark 13:19-20*

• Why does Jesus warn of great trouble?

Jesus wants us to keep strong when terrible things happen! Christians look forward to Jesus' return. However, we must be ready first to go through very hard times.

Mark wrote to Christians who faced terrible times in their lifetime. The Roman army would destroy Jerusalem. Many Christians would die for Jesus. Perhaps they thought that there would be no Christians left. But God looks after his people (his 'elect', NIV). He has chosen them and he will keep them.

> ⟫ *We must remember that too. Terrible times will come, but God is in control. He has told us that big trouble will come before Jesus comes back. We must keep on to the end.*

DO NOT BELIEVE EVERYTHING!
📖 *Mark 13:21-23*

• How do you know if a teacher is true or false?

• If someone says he is the Messiah, should we believe him?

• If someone says he is a prophet, should we believe him?

• If someone does a miracle, should we believe him?

We must test everything by the Bible. Jesus warns us that false teachers will come. He tells us that some teachers will say: 'Jesus has come back'. You may think that they are good people. They may do miracles. They may tell good stories. They may tell you that the Christian life is easy. But they 'deceive' people. That means they make people believe lies.

[This is very important. Many Christians are too quick to believe things. Teach your listeners how to know when teaching is wrong. You could talk about the wrong teaching that your listeners may hear. Ask them if these things are what the Bible says.]

> ⟫ 📖 *Mark 13:5, 23. Jesus tells us to watch out. There is real danger. When terrible times come, Jesus wants us to keep on to the end. He does not want us to believe lies. He wants us to trust **him**, even though it is hard.*

56 JESUS WILL COME BACK

◉ Background

Jesus wants his **disciples** to be ready for the terrible events of **the year AD 70.**

Jesus wants all **Christians** to be ready for the **end of the world.**

We must not be too afraid when terrible things happen. They do not mean that the end of the world has come. We must not believe people who say things like that. We must keep on with our Christian lives. We must trust Jesus.

So how **do** we know when Jesus will come back? Jesus now tells us what will happen; 📖 *Mark 13:24-37.*

◉ Main point

Jesus has promised! He will come back.

⊠ Something to work on

It is hard to believe that Jesus may come soon. It feels as if he will never come. We think that we will die first! Even if we do die, we need to be ready for him.

The devil wants us to forget that Jesus will come back. How can you help your listeners to remember?

◉ Notes

• **Mark 13:24-25.** This shows that Jesus will come to **judge.** These words are like words in the Old Testament. The prophets say that God will come like this. They show that God will come to **judge.** For example: Isaiah 13:9-11; Joel 2:10, 31.

• **Mark 13:26.** This is like Daniel 7:13-14. Jesus will come as the King and the Judge. Everyone will worship him.

• **Mark 13:30.** Jesus promises that these things will happen soon. The disciples will still be alive. Jesus must mean all the events of the **first** judgement, in the year AD 70. Great trouble will come soon. He wants his people to be ready for it.

JESUS WILL RETURN

>> *Jesus* **will** *come back. What do you think about that? Are you frightened? Do you want him to come soon?*

1. HE WILL COME BACK TO JUDGE THE WORLD

📖 ***Mark 13:24-26.*** These things are very frightening. Jesus will return to judge the world. He will come with all his power and glory. Everyone will know that Jesus is King. Everyone will fall on their knees to worship him. Then it will be too late to ask Jesus to forgive us. 📖 ***Revelation 6:12-17.***

>> *Are you ready for that day? Ask Jesus* **now** *to forgive you. Serve him* **now** *as your King.*

2. HE WILL COME BACK FOR HIS PEOPLE

📖 Mark 13:26-27. If you know Jesus, you do not need to be afraid! He has not come to punish you! He will come for his chosen people ('elect', NIV). He will take them home with him!

⊕ *What do you look forward to? (Example: birthday, visit of a friend...) How do you feel when you think about it?*

>> *This is much better than that! Your best Friend is coming! Think about it! Look forward to that great day! Pray for Jesus to come!*

LEARN FROM THE FIG TREE
📖 *Mark 13:28-31*

• What do people say when the fig tree starts to grow leaves?

The fig tree does not lie. The leaves mean that summer will soon come.

We do not know when Jesus will come back (Mark 13:32). However, we can tell when things start to change. Jesus wants us to watch out. He wants us to be ready.

It will be like it was for the first Christians, before Jerusalem was destroyed in the year AD 70. Christians will suffer more. False teachers will say many strange things. They will do miracles. **Then** we will know that Jesus will come soon.

Remember, Jesus does not lie! 📖 ***Mark 13:31.*** We may think that Jesus will never come. But he certainly will.

[You could talk about the Flood. No one believed Noah. But the judgment came and the people were not ready. 2 Peter 3:3-9 helps us to see why Jesus has been a long time.]

127

57 BE READY FOR JESUS

▣ Background

See ▣ **BACKGROUND** for Mark 13:24-31.

Jesus wants us to learn one big lesson in Mark 13. **He wants us to be ready for him**. This last section is the main point of Mark 13.

📖 *Mark 13:32-37*. Jesus says a lot more about this in **Matthew**. Jesus wants us to be ready for him! What does this mean?
📖 *Matthew 24:36-44*. (Matthew 25 is also about this.)

▣ Main point

Jesus will come back. Be ready for him.

⊡ Something to work on

Jesus tells us to 'watch' for his return. Jesus does not mean us to stop work! He wants us to wait for him, but he does not want us to do nothing! Jesus has work for us to do before he comes back. He wants us to take the good news to everyone in the world (Mark 13:10).

▣ Notes

• **Mark 13:32.** Jesus is God. However, while Jesus was on earth, he did not know everything, like God. He chose not to know everything, so that he could be a real human too. While Jesus was on earth, he did not know when he would return.

• **Mark 13:36.** 'sleeping' (asleep). Of course, we all need to sleep at night! Jesus uses sleep as a **picture** of our Christian lives. If we forget about Jesus, we are 'sleeping.' If we make things in this life too important, we are 'sleeping.' If we are lazy for God, we are 'sleeping'.

NO ONE KNOWS!
📖 *Mark 13:32-35*

⊕ *Imagine that your boss gives you a big job to do. Then he goes away. He promises to return one day to see how well you have worked. However, after one week he has not come back. You begin to work less hard. After one month, he still has not returned. Somebody said that he would come tomorrow. But he did not come. So now you only work when the weather is good. After one year he still has not come. You think that he will never come back. So now you rest and play games. You do not work at all. Suddenly your boss comes back. What will he say to you?*

This is like Jesus' story. If we knew when Jesus will return, then perhaps we would be ready. But we do not know when he will come. We become tired. We think that he will never come.

But he **will come**. And he wants us to be ready.

> ⏵ *No one knows when Jesus will come! So what about the people who say that they **do** know? Jesus says that they are wrong.*
>
> *No one knows when Jesus will come. Therefore, we must always be ready. Are you ready today?*

SO BE READY!

1. WATCH!
📖 *Mark 13:35-37*

Jesus wants us ready and awake like a security guard. If anything happens, a guard will see it. So what does this mean for us?

• Think and pray about Jesus' return.

• Remember what Jesus says will happen.

• Be ready for great difficulty.

2. WORK!
📖 *Mark 13:34*

• What work has Jesus given Christians to do?

• What work do you do for Jesus? Do you work well for him?

[You could tell Jesus' story in Matthew 25:14-30.]

> ⏵ *Are you 'asleep'? Have you forgotten that Jesus will come back? Are you busy with your own things? Then wake up! Watch and work! Be ready for Jesus.*

58 PREPARING FOR JESUS' DEATH

▣ Background

It is nearly time for Jesus to die. It is Wednesday. Jesus will die on Friday. The disciples still do not believe that Jesus will die. In Mark 14, Jesus helps them to prepare for his death.
📖 *Mark 14:1-42.*

📖 *Mark 14:1-11.* How do the different people prepare for Jesus' death (The Jewish leaders, the woman, Judas)?

(Mark loves to put different things together to make us think. See how Mark 14:1-2 is like Mark 14:10-11. In the middle is Mark 14:3-9. See how **different** it is.)

☉ Main point

Jesus' death is good news! How much do you love Jesus?

✲ Something to work on

We would not have wanted Jesus to die! **We** are not like Judas! But perhaps we are. There are many people like Judas. They look like Christians, but are not Christians inside. They love money, or something else, more than they love Jesus. Ask God to help you to talk about this.

☉ Notes

• **Mark 14:1.** 'Feast of Passover and Unleavened Bread.' This feast helped the Jews to remember how God saved them from Egypt. Then they had to kill a young sheep and put its blood over the door. God's angel killed Egyptian boys, but 'passed over' the houses that had blood on. Jesus is like the Passover lamb. He died (at Passover time) to save us from God's anger (Exodus 12:1-30).

• **Mark 14:3.** 'A woman.' John tells us that she was **Mary**, who lived in Bethany, with Martha and Lazarus (John 11:1-2, 12:1-7).

• **Mark 14:4-5.** John tells us that **Judas** said this. Probably he was the first to speak. Judas looked after the money, and he was a thief! (John 12:4-6)

• **Mark 14:3, 8.** The woman did something very special. People put 'perfume' on to make them smell nice. This perfume cost a year's wages! Probably she believed that Jesus was going to die. She wanted to show her big love for Jesus while she could. Nobody would be able to put perfume on Jesus' body when he died. But Jesus said that Mary had already done that!

READY TO KILL JESUS
📖 *Mark 14:1-2, 10-11*

- Do you know anyone who loves money more than they love Jesus?

- Do you know anyone who said that he was a **Christian**, or a **pastor**, because that way he could get more money?

Judas was never a true believer (John 13:10-11). Judas pretended to love Jesus. He seemed like all the other disciples. However, he loved money, not Jesus. So when the woman poured all her perfume over Jesus, he was very angry. What a waste of money!

Then Judas thought of another, terrible way to earn some money. 📖 *Mark 14:10-11.*

> ⨠ *Judas was willing to kill Jesus for money. What are **you** willing to do? Would you cheat to get more money? Would you try not to pay taxes? Would you only give a little money for Jesus? Are you sure that you love Jesus more than money? Do not pretend to be a Christian, like Judas!*

READY TO LOVE JESUS
📖 *Mark 14:3-9*

Jesus is ready to die. Look how he talks about his death. 📖 *Mark 14:8-9.* We do not like to talk about death, but Jesus does not mind! He calls it the 'gospel', the good news!

> ⨠ *Now we sing about Jesus' death – we know that it is good news. We love Jesus because he died for us and rose again. This is the best thing Jesus did. [Sing some songs to praise Jesus (at the end of the talk).]*

Most of Jesus' friends are not ready for Jesus to die. They do not understand why he must die. But Mary understands a little. She knows that she must show her love for Jesus while she can.

- How much did Mary love Jesus?

I think that I may have poured a **little** perfume over Jesus. I would save the rest for myself. But Mary did not care how much the perfume cost. **Jesus** was everything to her.

> ⨠ *We know much more than Mary did. We know that Jesus died on the cross to take away our sin. We should love him even more than Mary!*

> ⨠ *Are you ready to love Jesus? How much? How will it show?*

59 THE LORD'S SUPPER

◉ Background

It is now Thursday. Jesus knows that he will die the next day. The disciples need to know that his death is **for them**. They need to know that it is God's plan. The Passover meal becomes the Lord's Supper.

📖 *Mark 14:12-26.*

◉ Main point

Jesus is ready to die. Each of us needs to trust in his death, in a personal way.

✶ Something to work on

Christians often share in the Lord's Supper. The bread and wine are very familiar to us. But do we truly understand what Jesus means here? What does Jesus want his disciples to understand?

◉ Notes

- **Mark 14:12.** 'Feast of Passover and Unleavened Bread.' This feast helped the Jews to remember how God saved them from Egypt. Then they had to kill a young sheep ('lamb') and put its blood over the door. God's angel killed Egyptian boys, but 'passed over' the houses that had blood on. Jesus is like the Passover lamb. He died (at Passover time) to save us from God's anger. **Exodus 12:1-30.**

- **Mark 14:12-16.** These careful instructions are probably because Jesus' life is in danger. Jesus wants to meet in secret with his disciples.

- **Mark 14:21.** Judas was not saved in the end. Jesus says how terrible it will be for him (John 17:12).

- **Mark 14:22-24.** Jesus often speaks in **pictures**. He does not mean that the bread is his physical body. He does not mean that the wine is his physical blood. But he does want us, by faith, to **take** the gift of his death for ourselves.

- **Mark 14:24.** 'Covenant' – an important promise. 'Blood' shows how serious it is. Jesus' death brings in the new covenant that the Old Testament promised. Jesus' blood is God's sure promise that he will save everyone who trusts Jesus' death.

- **Mark 14:25.** Jesus wants the disciples to know that his death is not the end! They will eat and drink with him in heaven.

JESUS IS READY TO DIE

⊞ *You have a test or exam. Or perhaps you have an interview for a job. What do you do before it happens? You prepare! You know that you need to be ready.*

*It is so much harder for Jesus. Jesus must go through the most difficult, painful test ever. And he is **ready**.*

- He is ready to eat the Passover meal with his disciples (Mark 14:12-16).

- He is ready for Judas to give him away ('betray' him) (Mark 14:17-21).

- He is ready to share a meal that is about his own death! (Mark 14:22-25).

[Talk more about these three things. Jesus is in control. He is ready to go 'just as it is written about him' (Mark 14:21).]

➤ *We are often like the disciples. We are weak and afraid. We find it hard to trust God's word. But **our Saviour** was so ready to die for us! He was willing to take all that pain. Love him!*

'TAKE IT!'

📖 *Mark 14:22*

Jesus is ready to die. He must die alone. Only Jesus can take our sins. However, Jesus wants his disciples to **join in**. His death is **for them**. So they must share this 'death' meal together. Jesus is saying: 'I will die, and it is for **you**. Take my 'body' and 'blood'. Join in with my death.'

[Talk about the Passover. Say how the Israelites had to join in. They had to eat the lamb. The lamb's blood was over their door. They were safe because they joined in.]

➤ *We must join in! We believe that Jesus died. But that is not enough. Jesus' death does not save everyone. We must take his death for ourselves. We must trust Jesus to save **us**. We are only safe if Jesus is **our** 'Passover Lamb'. [Explain that we must not take the Lord's Supper until we have trusted Jesus in this personal way.]*

*When Christians have the Lord's Supper, we must be careful. It must not just be a habit. We must think what it means. As we eat and drink, we trust Jesus' death to take away our sins. We remember that Jesus' blood shows God's 'covenant' – he **promises** to save us and to bless us.*

60 THE BIG TEST

▣ Background

The time has come for Jesus to die. Jesus has prepared his disciples, but are they ready? Mark shows us the difference between the **disciples** and **Jesus**.

📖 *Mark 14:27-31*. The disciples **say** that they are ready for anything – even death.

📖 *Mark 14:32-42*. Jesus **prays**, so that he is ready for the cross.

This talk will be on Mark 14:32-42. We will come back to Mark 14:27-31 later, when we see what happens to Peter. 📖 *Mark 14:66-72*.

⊙ Main point

Jesus chooses his Father's will and takes up his cross. What will we choose?

✦ Something to work on

This section is about **Jesus**. We want to praise and love Jesus. He was willing to take all that pain for his people!

However, Mark also wants to show us **the disciples**. That makes us ask if **we** are ready for pain. There is always pain when we follow Jesus. 📖 *Mark 8:34-35*. Every day we choose. Will we take the hard way, like Jesus, or 'sleep' like the disciples? [Think of examples for your people.]

▣ Notes

• **Mark 14:35-36.** Mark has shown us how ready Jesus is to die. Many times, Jesus has said that he has come to die. Jesus has **not** changed his mind here. But it is so painful! So he cries out for some other way. However, **most of all**, Jesus wants to do his Father's will.

• **Mark 14:36.** 'Cup' or 'cup of suffering'. 📖 *Psalm 75:8*. We all deserve to drink God's cup of anger. Now Jesus must drink the cup of God's anger against **our** sin. For Jesus, the most painful thing about the cross is **his Father's anger**.

• **Mark 14:38.** 'The spirit is willing' – the disciples **want** to keep with Jesus (Mark 14:31). 'But the body/flesh (human nature) is weak' – they need to pray because they need God's help. (In Mark 14:42, the time has come and the disciples are not ready!)

JESUS SAYS YES TO THE CROSS

1. JESUS FEELS THE PAIN
📖 *Mark 14:33-36*

⊕ *Imagine having to drink strong, bitter poison. It tastes very bad and as hot as fire. And you must drink it all – a big cup!*

Jesus has to drink something much worse than that. He is going to the cross. For Jesus, the cross is like a cup full of God's burning anger. A cup full of God's curse. A cup full of the punishment of hell. This is because Jesus will take on our sins. He will take the punishment that we deserve (1 Peter 2:24).

• How does Jesus say he feels?

Jesus feels pain just as we feel pain. So he tells his Father how he feels. He cries out in his pain and fear. The cross is so terrible that Jesus longs for some other way.

2. JESUS SAYS YES
📖 *Mark 14:36*

⊕ *Do you sometimes say 'yes' because you did not really think about it? Afterwards you wish that you had said 'no'!*

Jesus saw how bad the cross would be. He knew everything that he would suffer. **And he still said yes!** Jesus really wanted not to have the pain. But he wanted even more to please his Father. Jesus must finish the plan to save us.

⟫ *Thank Jesus that he was willing to face so much pain. Love Jesus! Praise Jesus! [Talk more about this. Help the people to understand how much he has done for us. You could have some time to sing or pray.]*

THE DISCIPLES SLEEP
📖 *Mark 14:37-42*

The disciples do not want to fail! Like Jesus, they also want to do God's will. However, they are very weak.

• How does Mark show us how weak the disciples are?

⟫ *Do you want to follow Jesus? Do you want to do God's will?* **That is not enough, because you are weak.**

When do you find it hard to do what Jesus wants? When the tests come, we need to:
• *pray. Every morning, pray that you will be ready to do hard things for Jesus.*

• *put our faith in Jesus, who said yes to the hardest thing ever.*

61 JESUS GOES TO HIS DEATH

Background

It is late on Thursday night. Jesus is ready to go to the cross. He has prayed. He has tasted the 'cup' of suffering and said yes. The disciples say that they are ready to go with Jesus. But they are weak. They have not prayed (Mark 14:27-42).

Now Jesus gets up to go to his death. *Mark 14:41-52.*

Main point

Jesus **gives** himself up to die. The disciples **save** their lives, and run away.

Something to work on

Remember that the disciples still had the wrong idea. They still hoped that Jesus would become a great king. They were willing to stay with Jesus and fight! However, they were not willing to follow someone who failed. They were not ready for Jesus to go to the cross. Think how we can be like them.

Notes

• **Mark 14:44.** Judas kissed Jesus to give Jesus away. There must be no mistake. It was dark. Perhaps not all the crowd knew Jesus.

• **Mark 14:47.** John 18:10 tells us that this man was Peter. The disciples were not cowards. They were ready to fight. However, when Jesus did not fight, they ran away. They were not ready to give up their lives for nothing!

• **Mark 14:48.** They treat him like an outlaw, a bad person who leads a revolution!

• **Mark 14:49.** They did not arrest Jesus in the temple, or in the day. Mark 12:12 says that they were afraid of the crowd.

• **Mark 14:49-50.** The Old Testament Scriptures said that all this would happen. Jesus knows this. *Mark 14:27* (Zechariah 13:7). *John 18:1-11.* This shows that Jesus was in control of his own arrest!

JUDAS GIVES AWAY JESUS' LIFE
📖 *Mark 14:43-45*

[Paint a picture in words. Help your listeners to imagine the scene.] This is all very wrong. The Jewish leaders have paid money to Judas. And they have paid money to bad people. They come at night to arrest the innocent Jesus. They hate Jesus so much that they are willing to do anything. He must die!

Jesus is ready for them. He is even willing for Judas to kiss him. What a terrible thing for Judas to do!

> ⏩ *We should not be surprised when religious people do very bad things! We should not even be surprised when some Christian leaders do very bad things. Why does this happen?*

JESUS GIVES HIS OWN LIFE
📖 *Mark 14:46-49*

We know that Jesus is ready to go. He has even gone to meet this bad crowd! We know that he has power to stop these people, or to call angels to kill them. Their swords and sticks can do nothing against Jesus' power! There is no need for the big crowd of rough people. Jesus **gives** himself to them. He **lets** them take him and tie him up.

📖 *Mark 14:27*. Jesus knows what the Old Testament says about him. In Zechariah 13:7, it says that **God** will strike the Shepherd. Jesus knows that this is **God's** will. (Jesus is the Good Shepherd. He is glad to give his life for his sheep. 📖 *John 10:11, 14-18*.

> ⏩ *How do you feel about this wonderful Jesus?*
>
> ⏩ *If you are not yet following Jesus, how does this help you to trust him?*

THE DISCIPLES SAVE THEIR LIVES
📖 *Mark 14:50-52*

None of us wants to be like Judas. He gave away his best friend! But are we happy to be like the other disciples? What were they like?

- They were willing to fight – but Jesus did not want them to.
- They had promised to stay with Jesus, but they ran away.
  📖 **Mark 14:29, 31.**

> ⏩ *Are you frightened of the cross, like the disciples? When other people laugh at you, will you stay with Jesus? Or do you run away from any trouble?*

Remember 📖 **Mark 14:27!** The sheep will run, because Jesus must take our sins on his own. But Jesus does still die for those scared sheep!

62 NOT GUILTY!

⊡ Background

The leaders of the Jews have arrested Jesus. They want to kill him. However, the Jews have no right to kill him, because the Romans rule the country. So now the Jews have to find Jesus guilty of doing something wrong. They must show the Roman ruler, Pilate, that Jesus should be put to death. 📖 *Mark 14:55-65, 15:1-5.*

Mark also wants us to notice Peter. Jesus will be accused, and Peter will be accused too. See how different Jesus and Peter are –
📖 *Mark 14:53-54, 66-72.*

⊡ Main point

No one can find anything wrong with Jesus. Jesus goes to his death because he says that he is the Christ (Messiah).

⊡ Something to work on

Try to teach three kinds of lessons from this section.

- We want to love Jesus for what he did.

- We want to be like Jesus when we have to suffer for him. (However, that does not mean that it is always wrong to speak up!)

- We want to be ready to meet Jesus the Judge.

⊡ Notes

- **Mark 14:55.** 'Sanhedrin' or 'Council'. This was the most important Jewish court.

- **Mark 14:58.** 📖 *John 2:19.* Jesus had not said that **he** would destroy the temple. Anyway, Jesus meant himself. They would kill **him** and he would rise again in three days.

- **Mark 14:62.** 📖 *Daniel 7:13-14.* Jesus often called himself the 'Son of Man'. Now he clearly shows what that means. He is the Christ, the Messiah. He will sit at God's right hand and come to judge the world.

- **Mark 14:63.** The high priest tore his clothes to show that he was very unhappy at what Jesus said. He thought that Jesus had spoken 'blasphemy'. Jesus had said things that only God could truly say. (Inside, the high priest is very **pleased**! At last, they have some reason to put Jesus to death!)

NOT GUILTY!
📖 *Mark 14:55-61*

In many countries people hate Christians, just as these Jews hated Jesus. People will make up lies about Christians, to put them in prison, or to kill them. *[Use a true story if you can.]* Praise God that Jesus knows how it feels! And pray for God's help. Pray for his people to keep faithful to him.

They could find nothing wrong!
[Talk about Jesus' life. It was so beautiful, so perfect. Every thought, every word, every action was good.]

These Jews tried very hard. Some people came to tell lies about Jesus. Some people changed the words Jesus said (Mark 14:58). But it was clear that none of their stories were true. Everyone knew that Jesus had done nothing wrong!

• What did Jesus say to all these things? 📖 *Mark 14:60-61.*

Jesus did not **need** to say anything. Everyone knew that he was innocent. This also reminds us why Jesus went to the cross. It was for sinners. We **are** guilty, and Jesus was willing to suffer in our place. 📖 *Isaiah 53:6-7.*

> ⏵ *How do you feel about Jesus when you see him here? How does that help, when people blame you for something that you did not do?*

GUILTY!
📖 *Mark 14:61-65*

There is one thing that Jesus is happy to say. He **is** the Christ.

• Why should Mark 14:62 make the high priest very afraid? (See ⏺ **Notes**)

But the high priest is not afraid! He is glad to have a charge against Jesus. Jesus has said things that only God can say. He is guilty! He must die! So they take away the Son of God, they spit on him, they hit him, they make fun of him.

Mark 14 shows clearly who truly **is** guilty. These men judge Jesus, but **they** are guilty. And one day they must face **their** Judge – Jesus!

> ⏵ *What Jesus says in Mark 14:62 is true. He is the Christ. He is the Judge. We will all see him when he comes again. He will judge every one of us.*
>
> ⏵ *So what will **you** do with Jesus? And what will he do with you?*

All this time, Peter watches (Mark 14:53-54). What will Peter do when they start to ask **him** about Jesus? And what about us, when people hate our Saviour? Are you glad to say that you follow Jesus? When you have done nothing wrong, are you happy to suffer for Jesus? Later, Peter wrote these words. 📖 *1 Peter 2:20-23.*

63 'I DO NOT KNOW HIM!'

◉ Background

Earlier in the evening, Jesus had warned his disciples that they would leave him. Peter did not believe it! He promised to stay with Jesus, even if he had to die! 📖 *Mark 14:27-31.*

Now the Jews have arrested Jesus. The disciples have run away. Peter has come back to see what will happen to Jesus. He watches the high priest question Jesus. 📖 *Mark 14:53-65.*

Now it is Peter's turn to answer some hard questions. 📖 *Mark 14:66-72*

◉ Main point

Not even Peter is strong enough to follow Jesus. We **all** need Jesus' death on the cross to save us!

◉ Something to work on

Fear of other people is very strong. We fear what they may do or say. We need to help each other with this. These Bible passages will help: 📖 *Proverbs 29:25; Matthew 10:28; 1 Peter 3:13-17.*

◉ Notes

• **Mark 14:27.** Jesus uses some words from Zechariah 13:7 in the Old Testament. They show that everything will happen as God planned. **God** will 'strike' (hit) the Shepherd (Jesus). And the sheep (the disciples) will run for their lives.

• **Mark 14:28.** Jesus has warned that they will run from him. But they will come back to him after he rises from the dead. He wants them to know that his death is not the end.

• **Mark 14:68.** 'Denied.' This means that Peter said it was not true. Look back to Mark 14:30-31. Peter said that he would never 'disown' Jesus (say that he did not know Jesus).

• **Mark 14:72.** 'Cock crows.' This is the loud noise that a male chicken makes – usually early in the morning!

PETER HALF-FOLLOWED JESUS

📖 *Mark 14:54*

Jesus never calls his people to follow him **a little bit**. Peter thought that he was close enough to still be with Jesus. He also thought that he was far enough away to be safe. Was he right?

> ⊘ *Are you like Peter? Perhaps you like to call yourself a Christian. But you are afraid of what people will think about you. Perhaps you try to be like everyone else. Jesus is watching you. He knows if you are ashamed of him.*

PETER SAID THAT HE DID NOT KNOW JESUS

📖 *Mark 14:66-71*

- Why did Peter say that he did not know Jesus?

- What was Peter afraid of?

[Help your listeners to think what they might be afraid of. When do we try to hide what we think about Jesus? Why?]

> ⊘ *In the end, Peter cursed and swore to show that he did not know Jesus. What have you done to hide your love for Jesus?*

PETER WEPT

📖 *Mark 14:72*

- Why did Peter cry? Because he had been **proud** (Mark 14:29-31). Because he had not **listened** when Jesus warned him. Because he had been **ashamed** of Jesus, who he loved…

> ⊘ *Have you cried, like Peter, because you made Jesus sad? Or are you still more worried about what other people think of you?*

Like Peter, **all** Christians have failed Jesus. We are all so weak and afraid at times. But remember why Jesus went to the cross. He went to die for sinners, for weak people who cannot save themselves. Jesus watched Peter fail. And Jesus knew that his death will pay the price of Peter's sin. Peter said some terrible things, but Jesus forgave him. Jesus had great work for Peter to do. In the end, Peter even died for Jesus.

> ⊘ *As you ask Jesus to forgive your sin, ask him to teach you lessons. Ask him to change you. Ask him to make you strong as he made Peter strong.*

64 KILL HIM ON A CROSS!

▣ Background

Through Thursday night, the Jewish leaders said things against Jesus. They tried to find something which they could punish Jesus for. At last, Jesus said that he is the Christ, the Son of God. The Jews said that this is blasphemy. They said that Jesus should die for this.

However, now they must go to **Pilate**, the Roman ruler. Only Pilate can give the order for Jesus' death. What crime will they accuse Jesus of?

Jesus has said that he is the Christ, which means King. But **Pilate** is the ruler of the Jews! The Jews want Pilate to believe that Jesus is a problem to him. If Jesus is a King, perhaps he will lead the Jews against Pilate! 📖 *Mark 15:1-15.*

▣ Main point

Jesus has done nothing wrong – and they kill him on a cross. Barabbas is guilty – and they let him go free.

✴ Something to work on

It is hard to understand why the crowds hated Jesus so much. It is hard to think that we would have shouted, 'Kill him!' But are we any better? What do we do with Jesus today? Why do most people still not want Jesus?

▣ Notes

• **Mark 15:1-5.** Again, Jesus is silent. He will not say that he is innocent (has done nothing wrong). He will say that he is the Christ, the King of the Jews (see Mark 14:60-62).

• **Mark 15:6-10.** Pilate is afraid of the Jewish leaders. So he is afraid to let Jesus go. He hopes that the crowds will do this for him. Surely, they will want Jesus to go free! At Passover time, Pilate always sets one prisoner free. Barabbas is a bad and dangerous man. He has made trouble on the streets and killed someone. Pilate thinks that the crowds will want Jesus, not Barabbas, to go free.

• **Mark 15:13.** 'Crucify him!' That means 'kill him on a cross!'

• **Mark 15:15.** Mark says very little about the terrible pain Jesus suffered. A Roman death was painful and slow. But this is not the main thing that Mark wants us to think about. The main thing is **why** Jesus was on the cross.

INNOCENT BUT KILLED
📖 *Mark 15:13-14*

✚ *Tell a story about an innocent person. The court finds him guilty. Everyone knows that he is innocent. But he still goes to prison. Why did this happen?*

Everyone knows that Jesus has done nothing wrong.

Pilate knows very well why they have brought Jesus to him.
📖 ***Mark 15:10.*** Pilate knows they have made up lies against Jesus (Mark 15:3-5). Jesus says that he is the King of the Jews, but Pilate is not worried. He knows that Jesus has done nothing against the Romans. So Pilate tries to set Jesus free (Mark 15:9, 12, 14). Jesus is innocent – but Pilate still hands him over to be killed on a cross. Mark 15:15. Pilate is afraid of the crowds and the Jewish leaders!

The crowds also know that Jesus is innocent. 📖 ***Mark 15:14.*** No one can say what crime Jesus is guilty of. They just shout louder for Jesus to die.

People today know that Jesus did not deserve to die. People say that Jesus was a good person.

> ➲ **Jesus** was innocent, but we are not innocent. Jesus died because of our sin.

BARABBAS, NOT JESUS!
📖 *Mark 15:6-12*

Think how Barabbas was so different from Jesus. (Jesus had healed people, Barabbas was a killer. Jesus was innocent, Barabbas was guilty…)

[Explain how Pilate wants the crowds to set Jesus free.] The people have a choice. Will they ask for Jesus, who has done so much good? Or will they choose Barabbas, who is a bad man?

It is hard to believe what they say. Be shocked! They know that Jesus has done nothing wrong. But they **hate** Jesus so much that they will kill him. Why?

> ➲ *It was as if the whole world put Jesus on the cross. The Jewish leaders, the Roman ruler and the ordinary people all agreed. But are you really any different?*
>
> *They chose Barabbas, not Jesus. This is because they loved evil and not good. Are you any better when you choose to sin? You did not put Jesus on a cross, but do you push him away from you? Perhaps you do not want Jesus, because you do not want to change. So are you better than these people?*
>
> *Jesus did nothing wrong! But he died in the place of bad people like Barabbas and us. Will you ask Jesus to forgive you and be your Saviour?*

65 THE SAVIOUR WHO NO ONE WANTS

▣ Background

Remember how Mark tells his story.

- Mark 1-8 is about **who Jesus is**.

- Mark 9-16 is about **why Jesus came**.

Jesus has told us many times that he came **to die for sinners.** Now, as we see this happen we are sad, because everyone is so unkind. Jesus suffers so much. But we are also **glad**, because Jesus **is doing what he came for**. Jesus carries out God's perfect plan on the cross. Praise him! 📖 *Mark 15:16-32.*

⊙ Main point

Jesus is the Saviour. But nobody wants him.

✶ Something to work on

This section is very serious. Pray for those who do not want the Saviour.

Try also to encourage the **Christians**. We want to praise and love Jesus. He saved us when we did not want him! He loved us when we hated him!

◉ Notes

- **Mark 15:17.** The soldiers dress Jesus up as a king, so that they can laugh at him. They make the king's 'crown' with a plant that has sharp thorns, to hurt Jesus' head.

- **Mark 15:21.** This tells us that Jesus is now too weak to carry his cross. He has already suffered a lot.

- **Mark 15:23.** 'Myrrh.' This was probably to stop some of the pain. However, Jesus was willing to take all the pain.

- **Mark 15:26.** They wrote what the 'crime' was, for everyone to see. They put Jesus on a cross because he was 'the King of the Jews'.

- **Mark 15:29, 32.** They 'hurled' or 'heaped' insults. This means that they said rude things.

NO ONE WANTS THEIR SAVIOUR

[Describe how the different groups make fun of Jesus. In what ways do they show what they think of Jesus? What does Jesus have to suffer?]

- The soldiers. 📖 **Mark 15:16-20**

- The people who passed by. 📖 ***Mark 15:29-30.***

- The Jewish leaders. 📖 ***Mark 15:31-32.***

- The two thieves. 📖 ***Mark 15:27, 32.***

Jesus only did good things. But no one here has a good word for Jesus. They all want to do away with him. No one wants their Saviour.

> ⊗ *Is that true today? What kinds of people laugh at Christians? What kinds of people want nothing to do with Jesus? What do people think of a Saviour who dies on a cross? What about you?*

JESUS REALLY IS THE SAVIOUR

As he hung on the cross, Jesus knew what we all thought of him. But he still loved us. He still loved the people who hit him and laughed at him. This was how to be their Saviour!

Think again about what they shouted at Jesus. Perhaps their insults were true!

- ***'King of the Jews!'*** 📖 **Mark 15:18, 26.** The soldiers had great fun as they laughed at Jesus. But Jesus really is the King who God promised. He is the King of the Jews. And he is the King of everyone else too.

> ⊗ *Many of us bow and worship Jesus as our King! We know that it is true and we love him! What about you? You may have sung many songs to Jesus. But have you truly worshipped the King yet?*

- ***'He saved others, but he cannot save himself!'*** 📖 **Mark 15:31.** That is true too! Jesus, the Saviour cannot come down from the cross. But only because he must save his people from their sin. The cross is the only way to save us. *[Talk more about this. Show how Jesus paid the price for sin (Mark 10:45). Talk about his great love.]*

> ⊗ *Can you say: 'Jesus did not save himself because he died to save **me'**? Will you praise Jesus because he **is** the Saviour, **your** Saviour?*

66 THE WAY TO GOD

◾ Background

Mark tells us at the beginning of his book that Jesus is the Christ, the Son of God. 📖 *Mark 1:1*. It was a long time before Peter and the disciples really believed this; 📖 *Mark 8:29*.

Now, as Jesus dies, even a Roman soldier can see the truth. 📖 *Mark 15:39*. Here, at the cross, is where we too see the truth about Jesus.

◉ Main point

Jesus died under God's anger, to bring us to God.

✦ Something to work on

People who are not Christians need to understand why Jesus died. This talk will help them. You could have a special meeting to invite people to hear this talk. You could ask a Christian to tell the story of how they trusted in Jesus' death.

◉ Notes

- **Mark 15:33**. 'Sixth hour' means midday. It was dark for three hours in the middle of the day. This cannot be an eclipse. In an eclipse, the moon hides the sun for a few minutes. God made the 'whole land' dark to make people think. In the Bible, darkness often means that God is angry (Isaiah 13:9-10).

- **Mark 15:34**. This cry shows that God's anger is on **Jesus**. Jesus knows that God has left him. ('Forsaken' or 'abandoned' means 'left') This is like hell for Jesus. God's anger is on Jesus. God punishes Jesus for the sins of his people.

- **Mark 15:35-36**. They do not understand what Jesus is saying. Or perhaps they still make fun of him. They pretend that Jesus calls for Elijah, the great prophet. This shows how blind many people still are.

- **Mark 15:38**. The temple was in another part of Jerusalem. Mark wants us to see what happened in the temple at the time Jesus died. The temple curtain was very high and very thick. Only God could tear that curtain from the top.

What did this mean? The curtain stopped people from going into the 'Most Holy Place'. God's presence was here. God is too holy for us. Sinful people cannot come close to him. (Only the High Priest, on Atonement Day, could ever go through that curtain into the 'Most Holy Place'.) But when Jesus died, God tore the curtain. Now the way to God is open. Jesus is the way for sinful people to come to God! (1 Peter 3:18)

JESUS TOOK GOD'S ANGER
📖 *Mark 15:33-34*

⊕ *Think of someone you are afraid of. Imagine that person is very angry with you. Imagine that person does what he wants to you.*

We have done wrong. God should punish us. *[Talk more about this.]* We need to find peace with God. Or, one day, God's full anger will come down on us.

Think about Jesus on the cross. He always pleased His Father. His Father has loved him perfectly, forever. Now the sky has gone dark. Imagine how frightening that feels for the crowds. But Jesus knows why it is dark. God's anger points at **him**. It is like going to hell. He cries out in great pain: 'Why have you left me?'

Jesus knew the answer. God's anger came down on Jesus because of our sin. God was angry at our sin. Jesus took the punishment that we deserved. *[Use a word picture to explain this. Talk about Jesus' wonderful love.]*

Where does that leave you today? There are two answers:

⟫ **You have trusted Jesus to take your sin.** *He has taken your punishment. You are free! God's anger will never come down on you. You love Jesus so much.*

⟫ **You have not yet asked Jesus to take your sin.** *God is still angry with you. You are in great danger of hell. It is time to ask Jesus to be **your** Saviour!*

JESUS OPENED THE WAY
📖 *Mark 15:37-39*

⊕ *What happens if paper gets close to fire?*

We can never get close to God. He is so holy and we are so sinful. He is like a fire that will burn us up.

*[Talk about the temple and the curtain. You could draw it, or make a model of it. You need to show how people could **never** get close to God.]*

Jesus came to change all that! When he died, Jesus opened the way for sinful people to come to God! God tore the temple curtain into two parts. This was a sign. It was like God shouting, 'The way to God is now open! Come to me through Jesus!'

Our **sin** is the reason that we cannot come to God. But Jesus came to take away that sin! His death on the cross opened up the way to God.

⟫ *Jesus' death is the best news for people like us! It has opened up the way to God. God now calls us to come to him, through Jesus! Will you do that? Or will you stay away from God?*

67 THEY SAW, THEY CARED

▣ Background

Jesus has died. The way Jesus died made the Roman officer sure that 'this man was the Son of God'. 📖 *Mark 15:39.*

In Mark 16, we read how Jesus rose from the dead. But first, Mark shows us that there was no mistake. Several people saw that Jesus was truly dead. 📖 *Mark 15:40-47.*

⊙ Main point

Not everyone left Jesus when he died. These people were important witnesses. They knew that Jesus truly died.

✦ Something to work on

We can learn important lessons from the women and Joseph. Pray that it will encourage Christians who are shy or afraid. Perhaps some of your listeners believe in Jesus, but they have not yet said so. Or they have not yet been baptised to show that they follow Jesus. Perhaps you can offer Bible studies to help them think more about this.

⊙ Notes

• **Mark 15:42.** The next day was the Sabbath (Saturday). Sabbath started on Friday evening. They needed to bury Jesus now, before the Sabbath began. (The Sabbath was the day of rest.)

• **Mark 15:43.** 📖 *Matthew 27:57-60; Luke 23:50-54; John 19:38.* Joseph was an important Jewish leader. All the other leaders had wanted to kill Jesus. It was hard for Joseph to stand against them. He was brave to care for Jesus' body.

• **Mark 15:44.** The 'centurion' (army officer) was the soldier in charge. He had probably seen many people die. He saw the way Jesus died. He knew that Jesus really was dead.

JESUS TRULY WAS DEAD

• Who was there to see that Jesus really died?

They all knew for sure that Jesus was dead. He had died quickly, but there could be no mistake. So Joseph lovingly buried the body.

Some people may like to believe that Jesus never died. If so, he never truly rose from the dead! But Mark carefully shows that several people saw the dead body of Jesus.

> ⏩ *Christians never need to be afraid of the facts. People may ask us difficult questions. But **they** need to face the truth. Jesus **did** die and rise from the dead. Those facts mean that everyone should believe in Jesus.*

PEOPLE WHO CARED

THREE WOMEN
📖 *Mark 15:40-41, 47*

The other disciples ran away. Only John came to the cross. But these women had followed Jesus and cared for him. Now, as Jesus died, they would not leave him. They stayed right to the end. They were there as Joseph buried Jesus. They wanted to know where Jesus was, so that they could come back.

> ⏩ *These women encourage us. We do not read that they **say** anything. But they **show** their love to Jesus. They stay with him when everyone else leaves Jesus. Do you love Jesus like that? How can you show it more?*

JOSEPH
📖 *Mark 15:43-46*

*[See ⏺ **Notes** to find out more about Joseph from Matthew, Luke and John.]*

• When do you find it hard to say that you believe in Jesus?

Joseph found it very hard! He only believed in Jesus in secret. The other Jewish leaders hated Jesus, and Joseph was too afraid to speak out.

Now that has changed. Jesus' death made the disciples afraid. But it made Joseph brave! He knows that he **must** show his love for Jesus. The other leaders will hate him. They may try to kill him. But it is time for Joseph to show what he believes. *[Talk more about what Joseph does.]*

> ⏩ *As you think about Jesus' death for people like us, does it make you love him? Does it make you brave? Is it time to show everyone that you believe in Jesus?*

68 JESUS HAS RISEN!

◉ Background

Mark has shown that –

- Jesus is the promised Christ, the Son of God.

- Jesus died on the cross, as he promised.

- His disciples understand that Jesus is the Christ. But they cannot understand that he has to die. And they do not expect Jesus to rise from the dead!

📖 *Mark 16:1-8.* (Some people believe that Mark ended his Gospel at Mark 16:8. Probably, someone added Mark 16:9-20 many years later.)

◉ Main point

Jesus rose from the dead, as he said.

⊡ Something to work on

Most of your listeners believe the facts. They know that Jesus has risen. But some still do not trust in him! How can you show them that this does not make sense?

⊕ *[You could use this word picture. Your house is on fire. You know that the door is the way to safety. You believe in the door. But you love your house too much. You do not go out through the door. What happens?]*

◉ Notes

- **Mark 16:1.** This is how the women show their love for Jesus. On Friday, there had not been much time. They could not care for Jesus' body as they wanted to.

- **Mark 16:5.** This was an angel. 📖 *Matthew 28:2-5.*

- **Mark 16:7.** 'just as he told you.' 📖 *See Mark 14:28.*

- **Mark 16:7.** Peter had said that he did not know Jesus. But Jesus is willing to forgive him. The women must tell Peter. Jesus wants Peter to be there in Galilee. (Galilee, by the lake, is where Jesus first called Peter to follow him.)

JUST AS JESUS SAID!
📖 *Mark 16:6-7*

⊞ Some things are very hard to believe. [*Tell a story about this. Perhaps you thought that something was impossible. You would not believe it. Then many things showed you that it happened. In the end, you had to believe the* **facts**.]

Everyone knows that dead men do not come back to life! These women did not even hope that Jesus would rise from the dead. They came to care for his dead body.

The facts are clear.

- Someone has rolled away the large stone.

- The tomb is empty.

- An angel tells them that Jesus has risen.

- Jesus had told them that this would happen.

> ⏩ *Jesus* **has** *risen from the dead. God wants us to be sure about the truth. Jesus has* **proved** *that he is the truth. He has risen! This means that –*
>
> • *Jesus is the only way to God.*
>
> • *everyone should trust in Jesus.*
>
> *Think – what will happen to people who will not believe the facts?*

THE WOMEN ARE STILL AFRAID
📖 *Mark 16:8*

These women have seen the empty tomb. An angel has told them that Jesus has risen. But they are still afraid! They still do not know whether to believe it!

> ⏩ *Are you like these women? You want to believe but you are afraid? Jesus is very kind. He will help you to believe.*

The disciples do not yet believe. These women do not fully believe. However, Jesus has a message for them. 📖 *Mark 16:7.* He wants to show them that he has risen. It really is true! And he wants to see **Peter**. Peter is ashamed. He has said that he does not know Jesus. Perhaps Peter thinks that Jesus will never forgive him. But he will!

> ⏩ *Perhaps you have been slow to believe. Perhaps you have said bad things about Jesus, like Peter.* **It is not too late to believe!** *The risen Jesus will forgive you. Come to him now.*

69 BELIEVE AND TELL!

⊡ Background

Mark probably did not write Mark 16:9-20. There are many good reasons to think this. However, Mark 16:8 does seem a strange place to end! Perhaps Mark was not able to finish. Probably, someone added Mark 16:9-20 many years later. (Many people who love God's word say this.)

However, this section is part of our Bible. We can still learn from it. Most of Mark 16:9-20 is in the other Gospels. We should be careful about the parts that are **only** found here (see ⊡ **Notes** on Mark 16:17-18).

This ending shows that the disciples were slow to believe. But Jesus still has a job for them! They must go and tell the world about the good news.

⊡ Main point

At last, the disciples believe! Now they must tell the world.

⊡ Something to work on

Mark tells his good news so that people will **believe**. 📖 *Mark 1:1, 15.* As you finish Mark, pray that everyone will see how important this is (Mark 16:16).

⊡ Notes

- **Mark 16:14.** The disciples should have believed those who had seen Jesus. So Jesus tells them off ('rebukes' or 'scolds' them).

- **Mark 16:16.** Baptism does not save anyone. Baptism does not even help to save anyone. However, someone who believes in Jesus will **show** that they believe. The Bible says that they should be baptised to show their faith.

- **Mark 16:17-18.** Jesus promises many gifts to his people. However, the rest of the Bible does not say that Jesus' people will be able to pick up snakes or drink poison. It does say that we should not do dangerous things to put God to the test (Matthew 4:5-7).

- **Mark 16:17, 20.** 'Signs' ('miracles'). Notice that these were not just miracles. They were miracles to **show that the message was from God.** This is what 'sign' means. A sign tells us something. (Why was there a special need for these signs? Why might it be different today? When might God do special miracles to show that his word is true?)

BELIEVE THE GOOD NEWS!
📖 *Mark 16:9-14*

⊕ *[Tell a story like this.] You have some good news. You tell people, but they do not believe you! How do you feel?*

• How many times in this section do we read that people did not believe?

The disciples are so sad that Jesus is dead! They cannot believe that he is now alive!

• What does Jesus think about this (Mark 16:14)?

It is very sad when we will not believe. Jesus has gone through all that pain for his disciples. He has died for their sins on the cross. He has risen from the dead. He has done all this for them and they will not believe that it is true!

⏵ *Are you like these disciples? How many times have you heard about Jesus? You know all the facts. You know that the Bible tells you the truth. But you still will not believe in Jesus. What does Jesus think about that?* 📖 *Mark 16:16.*

TELL THE GOOD NEWS!
📖 *Mark 16:15*

⊕ *When you have good news, do you keep it quiet? No, you tell everyone!*

Now imagine that your good news will affect many people. Perhaps you found a good medicine for AIDS. Would you keep it secret? That would be so wrong!

Jesus tells the disciples to go and tell the world about him! The disciples are the beginning of Jesus' church. So this command is for us today. The world still needs to hear the good news. Who, in your country, does not know the truth about Jesus? What other countries need to hear about Jesus? What does your church do to help tell the world the good news?

⏵ *We can have many excuses. Perhaps we are afraid, or busy, or lazy. We find it hard, because people do not want to know about Jesus. The disciples did not find it easy! Some people hated them and killed them!*

⏵ *If you love the good news, you will want to tell other people. If you love Jesus, you will want to obey him. Think and pray about how to do this.*

📖 **Mark 16:20.** Jesus, in heaven, 'worked with them'. Jesus did his great work. He came to die and rise again. Now his people must do the work he has given them. **And Jesus works with us!** We are not alone. As we tell the good news, Jesus gives eternal life. Praise him!

E. How to use Preaching Mark
Worked Example

Before you preach you need to study hard and pray. Ask God to help you understand this Bible section.

The first thing to do is to **Read Mark 2:13-17.** Remember the story so far. Think how Mark 2:13-17 fits into the story. The **Background** notes will help you think about this.

Notes

These will help you to understand difficult things in the section. You may need to explain some of these things to the people.

Main point

Read the section again and again until you understand it all. Try to understand the main thing that it teaches. This will be the main point of your talk. Try to understand why it is very important for your people. Pray that they will understand it clearly.

- *Do you understand why it was a shock for Jesus to call Levi?*
- *How does this connect with Mark 2:17?*

So the main point of the section is this: **Jesus did not come for good people. He came for sinners.**

? STUDY: Mark 2:13-17

7 THE KIND OF PEOPLE WHO JESUS CALLS

◉ Background

In Mark 2:1-12 Jesus shows that he has the power to forgive sins. So now, Jesus shows that he did not come for good people. He came for sinners. Jesus came for people who need him to forgive their sins.

Mark 2:17 is the second time that Jesus tells us **why he came.** (See Mark 1:38.)

◉ Main point

Jesus did not come for good people. He came for sinners.

◉ Something to work on

People still think that Jesus chooses good people! Most people think that they are good people! They think that Jesus is pleased with them because they are good people. This section teaches that this is **wrong.** You need to think and pray how to say this.

You want bad people to see that Jesus came for them! You want them to ask Jesus to save them from their sin.

Some people think that they are already good. You want them to see

that they are bad. You want them to ask Jesus to make them good.

◉ Notes

- **Mark 2:14.** 'Levi' is another name for **Matthew.**

- **Mark 2:14.** 'Tax collectors.' These were Jews who collected taxes for the Romans. Most people hated tax collectors, because they worked for the Romans. They thought that a true Jew would never help the Romans. Most tax collectors were also cheats. They became rich because they kept too much money for themselves.

- **Mark 2:15.** 'Sinners.' We know that everyone is a sinner. But the Jews called only some people 'sinners'. These were people who lived a bad life. For example, the Jews called prostitutes 'sinners'. Tax collectors and 'sinners' were often friends. The Jews hated them all.

- **Mark 2:16.** 'Pharisees.' They were people who tried very hard to keep God's laws. They were very strict. They thought that they were good people.

28

Something to work on

People still think that Jesus chooses good people! Most people think that they are good people! They think that Jesus is pleased with them because they are good people. This section teaches that this is **wrong.** You need to think and pray how to say this.

You want bad people to see that Jesus came for them! You want them to ask Jesus to save them from their sin.

YOUR TALK

You are now ready to prepare your talk in your own language. The ideas that we give you will help you. You must make it your own talk that comes from your heart. Ask God to help you. Write some notes in your own language.

Starting your talk

Think how to start your talk so that people understand what it is about. Help them to see why it is important for them. Here is one idea:

Do you like surprises? [Give some examples.] *Jesus often surprises us! In today's Bible section Jesus did the opposite to what everyone expected. Some people loved it! Other people hated it! I wonder if Jesus will give you a good surprise today.*

Or perhaps it will be a hard shock.

Imagine that you were in the crowds that day. In that crowd were many people who wanted to hear Jesus. You all listened to Jesus teaching, by the lake. But Jesus did not call any of you to follow him and be his special disciple. Then Jesus saw someone who was very busy. He was too busy to come to hear Jesus. What was he doing? He was making lots of money! But Jesus stopped and said: 'Follow me!' What a surprise! What a shock! Why did Jesus want someone like Levi!

You can talk more about Levi and about why people hated him. Imagine how disappointed people were that Jesus chose this bad person!

In this section, there are three important truths to teach. These truths all help to explain the main point. They show how Jesus came for sinners.

1. JESUS CALLS SINNERS

📖 *Mark 2:17*

• *Are you the kind of person Jesus calls?*

• *Are you a sinner?*

Talk about the kind of person Levi was. Talk about the group Jesus was happy to eat with. Try to imagine it in your town or village. Notice what Mark 2:17 says. It does not say that Jesus looked down on these people. It says that Jesus **came** especially for them.

This is good news for bad people! No one else cared about Levi! Everyone hated all these 'sinners' and tax collectors. But Jesus came for the worst people! He loved them! Talk more about this.

This is bad news for good people! Notice who Jesus did **not** come to call (Mark 2:17). 'Righteous' people are good people. The Pharisees think they are good enough already. They are not happy for Jesus to eat with bad people! 📖 *Mark 2:16.*

Talk more about this. People today, who think they are good, will look down on bad people. They do not like it when Jesus says that he came for sinners.

This is important for saved people! If

Jesus has forgiven us, we will want to tell others about Jesus. So what kind of people will we tell? Will we only tell nice people, or people who go to church? Or will we tell people who we think are bad?

2. WHY JESUS CALLS SINNERS

📖 *Mark 2:17*

The Pharisees found this hard to understand. How can a teacher like Jesus choose to go to the bad people? Perhaps we too find it hard to understand. Surely, Jesus likes best the nice people who go to church and are kind to their neighbours?

*Jesus explains why he came for sinners. It is because they **need him!*** Use Jesus' picture of a doctor to help your people understand this. Show how only sick people go to the doctor. Tell your people about Jesus, who can make all their sins better. Tell them how he died on the cross to do this. They must ask Jesus to forgive all their sin and make them truly good people.

Also, show your people why 'good' people do not want Doctor Jesus. They think they are good, so they do not want him to forgive their sins. Tell them a story about a healthy woman who visits the doctor. She tells him all about how

---

➡ PREACH: Mark 2:13-17

JESUS CALLS SINNERS

📖 Mark 2:17

Are you the kind of person Jesus calls? Are you a sinner? *[Talk about the surprise of what Jesus says. Jesus came for sinners!!]*

• **This is good news for bad people!** Everyone hated all these 'sinners' and tax collectors. But Jesus came for the worst people! He loved them!

• **This is bad news for good people!** See who Jesus did **not** come to call (Mark 2:17). 'Righteous' people are good people. The Pharisees think that they are good enough already. They are not happy for Jesus to eat with bad people (Mark 2:16)!

• **This is important for saved people!** If Jesus has forgiven us, we will want to tell others about Jesus. So what kind of people will we tell? Will we only tell nice people, or people who go to church? Or will we tell bad people?

WHY JESUS CALLS SINNERS

📖 Mark 2:17

Jesus explains why he came for sinners. It is because they need him! *[Use Jesus' picture of a doctor to help your people understand this.]* Only sick people go to the doctor. Jesus can make all our sins better. He died on the cross to do this. Ask Jesus to forgive all your sin and make you well.

[Also, show why 'good' people do not want Doctor Jesus. They think that they are good already! They do not need him to forgive their sins.]

⊕ Tell a story about a healthy woman who visits the doctor. She tells him all about how well she is! She does not let the doctor examine her. She does not need that! She just wants him to be pleased with her! Of course, the doctor will not waste his time with healthy people! Jesus did not come for 'good' people, because they do not need a Doctor.

WHAT JESUS CALLS SINNERS TO DO

📖 Mark 2:14

Levi loves money. Jesus calls him away from his money. He follows Jesus. *[Show the people how this is a complete change of life for Levi.]*

Jesus calls us to leave behind our wrong way of life. He calls us to leave our sins. He calls us to turn round and follow Jesus.

⯈ *Tell a story about a person who does not take the medicine which the doctor gives her. Will she get better?*
⯈ *Will you take the medicine that Jesus gives? Will you ask him to forgive you and leave your wrong way of life?*

29

---

well she is! She does not let the doctor examine her. She does not need that! She just wants him to be pleased with her! Of course, the doctor will not spend his time with healthy people! Jesus did not come for 'good' people, because they do not think that they need a doctor.

You may add something else to your story. Two months later, the woman died. She had a disease inside. She was not truly well. She needed the doctor to examine her. Now it was too late. Good people do really need Jesus. They are sinners too. Ask your people to go to

Doctor Jesus for a health check. They must ask Jesus to show them their sin.

3. WHAT JESUS CALLS SINNERS TO DO

📖 Mark 2:14

Imagine you are Levi. The one thing you care about is **money.** *You have lost all your friends for money. You have spent your life cheating people for money. Now Jesus says 'Follow me!' That is a very big thing to ask! But what does Levi do? He leaves his life behind and follows Jesus. That is a change of direction. Levi was going one way and now he turns round and goes the other way!*

Jesus calls us to leave behind our old life. He calls us to leave our sins. He calls us to turn round and follow Jesus.

It is important for your people to understand this. Jesus did not come just to be with sinners. He came to save us from our sin. He came to change our lives. Use a word picture like this one:

Imagine that you go to your doctor. He tells you what is wrong. He gives you the medicine to take. Then you put the medicine away. You do not take it. Will you get better? Of course you will not!

Jesus gives us the medicine. It is free! He says: 'I will forgive your sins.' He says: 'leave your sins and follow me'. Will you take the medicine?

Finish your talk

• *What do you want people to remember?*

• *What do you want them to do?*

• *Tell them again the main point.*

• *Perhaps they need some time to pray quietly.*